The
Real
Thing

Fabric printing
by hand

STEPHEN RUSS

Fabric printing by hand

Watson-Guptill Publications
New York

To my students
who asked all the questions
and gave some of the answers

PUBLISHED MCMLXIV BY STUDIO VISTA LIMITED, LONDON
PUBLISHED MCMLXV BY WATSON-GUPTILL PUBLICATIONS, INC, NEW YORK, NEW YORK
AMERICAN EDITION EDITED BY JACK CLOONAN
PRINTED IN GREAT BRITAIN BY STAPLES PRINTERS LTD, ROCHESTER, KENT
LIBRARY OF CONGRESS CATALOG CARD NUMBER: 64-21986

Contents

List of illustrations

Introduction

The craft of fabric printing contains within itself the attributes common to all printing processes. As a convenience it makes possible the production of a large number of identical transfers from an original image. As an art it allows the construction of formal order and the demonstration of the evocative properties of the materials used.

The etcher and the lithographer make their prints on paper, each print an individual, complete and self-sufficient. The fabric printer puts down his prints side by side on a continuous length of cloth. For him the complete statement is the piece of cloth, and the separate prints are no more than units adding up to a composite whole. The designer who comes to fabric printing from one of the other printing crafts often finds it difficult at first to adjust his mind to the special problem of designing for a continuous length. It is indeed a difficult problem.

A drawing may be satisfactory on its own, conceived within and supported by a rectangular frame which isolates and limits its area. But if the frame is removed and the drawing surrounded by an expanse of identical repetitions of itself, the situation changes. The formal relationships which were meaningful in the original drawing are now upset and replaced by something unintended. The original focus may now find itself subordinate to some marginal area which has been reinforced in the act of repetition, and the lines of stress in the original may be supplanted by an unexpected and capricious new association. The ground may become the figure. These troubles will tend to disappear when once the designer has learnt to think of the piece of cloth as a whole, and this means to think in rhythm. The act of printing is by nature rhythmical, and this is the nature of the craft. As in music, the beat may be simple or compound, hidden or exposed, but it is always there.

All the hand printing processes can be called intermittent or discontinuous, to distinguish them from the continuous flow which comes through the rollers of a printing machine. The block printer has to ink up his block with a fresh charge of colour for each impression, the screen printer has to lift his screen from the cloth and lower it into the next position. The consequence of this can be seen in any piece of hand printed material.

No human being can ever repeat any action exactly, and no hand printer can achieve perfect alignment in all the impressions right down the cloth, nor can he achieve an absolutely equal application of colour. There will always be a small irregularity or shimmer in the total appearance. This is not to say that fecklessness and incompetence will do; far from it. The irregularity should be no more than a master bricklayer would allow himself. Quite apart from this small incidental irregularity, there is no reason why the hand printer should not set out from time to time to produce works which are openly and admittedly random. The medium is very versatile, and there are many ways in which this can be done. Here is one territory in which the hand printer enjoys a clear advantage over the machine.

The materials of the craft are fabric and dye; and fabric is not the same thing as paper, nor is dye the same thing as paint. To understand what these materials are and what they can do, they must be handled. Pottery cannot be learnt at the drawing board and neither can fabric printing. The most obvious material property of woven fabrics is their flexibility. Although they can be stretched out hard and flat we think of them more familiarly as something soft and folded. Any decoration, whether printed or woven, will run with the fabric, in and out of the folds, sometimes in shadow, sometimes upside down, foreshortened and overlapped, at no time looking like a piece of paper pinned to a drawing board.

The whole study of dyes is a formidable task even for an organic chemist, and is certainly outside the scope of the ordinary hand printer. Nevertheless the printer must understand that his work involves the control of a chemical reaction. The ingredients in his recipe may be colourless solids or liquids. He must learn to weigh and measure accurately and to perform a sequence of operations leading up to the development of the colour in the fabric. He will have to learn to manage gradations of tone and colour by calculation and not by eye.

Before the different processes are introduced one by one it must be made clear that each has its own unique and special quality. A thrown pot is not the same as a coiled pot, and tie-dyeing is not the same as batik. The artist will understand this intuitively. For the beginner it would be best if he could approach each process with an open mind and, at first, let it teach him.

All the processes mentioned in this book can be practised by the amateur at home; some will take up more time and more room than others. Screen printing, for instance, requires the exclusive use of a table during the printing, tie-dyeing can be picked up and put down like knitting. None of the special apparatus need be expensive, and most of it can be improvised from very humble raw materials. The techniques have been made as simple as it is possible to make them without taking any improper short cuts.

Any technique omitted is omitted because it depends on equipment beyond the resources of the amateur. The aim, rather, has been to show just how much can be done on the kitchen table.

1 · Textile fibres and fabrics

One of the properties that distinguish dye from paint is a certain selectivity. Paint can be applied to practically any kind of surface; dyes tend to have a natural preference or affinity for a particular type of fibre. If they are applied to a fibre for which they have no affinity, they will be rejected, and dyeing will not take place. It is, therefore, important for the dyer and fabric printer to know something about the material on which he is working.

The natural fibres are classed under two descriptive headings, animal and vegetable. Animal fibres include wool and natural silk. Vegetable fibres include cotton, linen, jute and the like. Some of the man-made fibres, such as viscose rayon, resemble the natural vegetable fibres very closely, and for this reason it would be better to use the more comprehensive word cellulosic to describe the whole of this group. Other synthetic fibres such as nylon, 'Terylene' (U.K.) and 'Dacron' (U.S.A.) are different altogether, and the amateur seldom attempts to print on them.

The first thing to do is to identify the fibres, and the simplest test is by burning. A thread of wool or natural silk held in a naked flame will give off an unmistakable smell of burning feathers. The thread will continue to char whilst it is held in the flame, but will go out as soon as it is withdrawn, forming at the end a black bead. The cellulosic fibres burn with a smell resembling charred paper. They continue to burn after withdrawal from the flame, and they form no bead. Unfortunately this test cannot take into account the complicated structure of some types of spinning and weaving. It is not uncommon to find a warp of one fibre and a weft of another, and sometimes a yarn may be spun from a mixture of different fibres. In such cases identification requires detailed testing with chemical stains. For the amateur working on a small scale it is usually more convenient to rely on the advice of a reputable and knowledgeable draper or fabric retailer.

Dyeing and printing are both influenced by the physical structure of the textile fabric, as well as by the chemical composition of the fibres from which it is made. For instance, a brushed cotton is more absorbent than unbrushed cotton. Weaves, such as twill, with a pronounced diagonal rib may give the block printer some trouble, as his colour may tend to settle on the ribs and miss the intervening grooves. Tie-dyers will find that thick material gives bold and open results, fine material fine results.

Before any work can be started, the fabric must be scoured to rid it of all impurities and dressings. These are likely to consist of the size added to the yarn as a preliminary to weaving, but there may also be some kind of filler added to the woven fabric. Most of the anti-crease finishes repel dyes.

9

Cotton and linen are boiled for half an hour in water containing a little soapless detergent such as Lissapol, Stergene or Teepol (U.K.); Duponol or Synthrapol (U.S.A.). Wool is washed for half an hour in a similar solution, but the temperature must be kept down to 40°C (105°F), and the material must not be rubbed or stirred vigorously or it will felt. Natural silk is boiled for an hour in water containing olive oil soap equivalent to ten per cent of the weight of the silk. In all cases the scouring process ends with a very thorough rinsing, after which the fabric is hung out to dry.

2 · The dyes

The distinction between paint and dye is something easily seen and felt. It comes from the difference in nature between the two substances. Paint consists of finely ground solid particles suspended in an adhesive binding medium. A coat of paint on a piece of fabric obliterates the natural lustre of the fibre, clogs the weave, and leaves the material dull, stiff and heavy. The particles of a dye are individual molecules, and these unite with the molecules of the fibre by an electrical bond. Dye leaves the material with its natural lustre and softness undiminished.

There would be no difficulty in preparing an assortment of coloured liquids from infusions of, say, charcoal, beetroot, spinach and the like, and trying them out on fabric, hoping to make a dye. The result of all such trials can almost certainly be predicted. At first the fabric would take up some of the colour from the infusion, but its hold would be weak. The colour given by charcoal and other suspended solids would be shed as the fabric was rubbed, the colour given by vegetable stains would come out in the wash. Even if the fabric was not washed the colour would be likely to change and fade under the influence of light and air. To qualify as a dye, a colour must be capable of such intimate association with the textile fibre that it cannot be removed by ordinary treatment such as rubbing and washing. To be a good dye, a colour must not change or lose its colour in the conditions of everyday use.

At one time or another all kinds of things have been used as dyes, insects and shellfish, the leaves, berries, bark and roots of plants. There can be little doubt that an even greater number must have been tried without success. Out of all the abundance of naturally occurring coloured solids and liquids it is remarkable how few have the property of dyeing textile fibres. Working by trial and error, the early dyers and printers stumbled, in the course of five thousand years, on fewer than one hundred natural dyes. It is not likely that this number would have been increased in another thousand years of groping. And yet today we have an expanding, world-wide dye manufacturing industry, and something like three thousand synthetic dyes on the market. This dramatic change follows directly from the work of the organic chemists who, in the 1850's, first began to unravel the dye molecule. With this understanding it became possible, at last, to create new dyes. The first synthetic dye –

the basic aniline colour 'Mauveine' – was made in 1856 by W. H. Perkin. He was only eighteen at the time.

For practical purposes the dyes are usually divided into classes, the system of classification being based, more or less, on the different modes of application. This is a working and not a chemical classification. The classes are as follows:

Direct dyes

These dyes are soluble in water and have a direct affinity for all the cellulosic fibres. Some of them will also dye natural silk and wool. All direct dyes may be applied either from the dyebath or by any of the printing processes. A very wide range of colours is available, and these can be mixed one with another to give compound shades. The colours are not outstandingly brilliant. Fastness to light varies from individual to individual, and ranges from poor to good. Fastness to washing is usually low.

This class of dyes is entirely man-made, and has no counterpart in nature. Nothing of the kind was known before 1884.

For his first attempts a beginner might well choose to work with the direct dyes. They are versatile, easy to use, and cheap. With them he will be able to practise dyeing and all the styles of printing. Once the mechanics of the craft have become familiar some attention can be diverted to learning new recipes.

Vat dyes

All vat dyes are coloured solids, insoluble in water and, as such, incapable of dyeing textile fibres. They all share one valuable characteristic; the ability to assume another form – known as the 'leuco' form – when treated with chemical reducing agents. In their leuco form all vat dyes become soluble in weak alkaline solutions, and in this way they can be introduced into textile fibres. The process of converting a vat dye into its leuco form in an alkaline solution is known as vatting, and the bath so made is a vat.

Dyeing takes place in two stages. In the first stage the fabric is immersed in the vat where it absorbs the dye in its leuco form. In the second stage the material is withdrawn from the vat and exposed to the air. The oxygen in the air regenerates the original colour as an insoluble precipitate within the fibre.

Natural indigo, extracted from the sap of *Indigofera tinctoria* and other leguminous plants, is the ancestor of this ancient family. The Egyptians were making indigo vats in 3000 B.C. Today we have indigo derived from coal tar, and in addition a number of related compounds known as indigoid, thioindigoid, and anthraquinoid vat dyes. All these compounds can be prepared as low temperature vats, and for this reason they are valued by batik workers and tie-dyers.

The vat dyes are used extensively as printing colours in industry, but they cannot be used in this way by the amateur because the fixation of the colour needs a special steam installation beyond the scope of domestic improvisation.

The vat dyes are used mainly on cellulosic fibres, but they will also dye silk and wool. The number of colours available is limited, and not all of these may be mixed together to give intermediate shades. In fastness to light and fastness to washing, vat dyes are unsurpassed.

Soluble vat dyes

One of the practical difficulties in handling ordinary vat dyes is that the reduced, or leuco compound is chemically unstable. The discovery of a stable salt of leuco-indigo was first made in 1920 by Bader and Sunder, and the product introduced to the trade two years later under the name Indigosol-O. Other workers were not slow to follow up with the stable leuco compounds of other vat dyes.

The soluble vat dyes are soluble in water or in weak alkaline solutions, and they may be applied from an ordinary dyebath, hot or cold. They may also be used as printing colours by the amateur without special apparatus. These dyes will dye cotton, silk and wool, and they inherit the general fastness properties of the vat colours from which they are derived.

Mordant dyes

The archetypal mordant dye is the crimson colour found in the root of the madder plant *Rubia tinctorum*. Decoctions of madder in boiling water will dye wool and silk, but will not dye cotton because madder has no natural affinity for the cellulosic fibres. To dye these fibres certain other substances, notably alum, must be present to assist the madder. The earliest surviving fragments of madder dyeing show that these assistants were used, even if the reason for using them was not understood. It used to be thought at one time that the action of these assistant chemicals was corrosive, pitting the surface of the fibre and thus opening the way for the dye to get inside. For this reason they were given the name mordants, from the French word *mordre*, to bite. A mordant is now considered to be a chemical with the ability to combine with a dye in such a way as to precipitate within the textile fibre an insoluble colour lake. A mordant dye is one that depends for its action on the presence of a mordant.

Frequently the same parent dye will be capable of combination with a number of different mordants, in each case giving a different final colour. Such dyes are said to be polymorphic, and madder is a good example. Madder and a battery of different mordants together maintained the whole calico printing trade throughout its golden era.

Mordant dyeing depends on bringing together dye, mordant and fibre in the conditions that will induce the desired precipitation of colour. The mordant may be applied first and the dye after, or the dye first and the mordant after. Or dye and mordant may be applied simultaneously.

Within this class is a group of dyes commonly known as chrome colours. They are essentially printing colours, and are not suitable for dyeing. Fixation of the printed material can be carried out at home. The range of available colours is wide, and within certain limits these colours may be mixed together to give intermediate shades. In fastness to light and to washing their performance is better than the direct dyes, not as good as the vats.

Basic dyes

The title 'basic' given to this group of dyes refers to their chemical nature: it does not mean that they are in any way fundamental or indispensable. The basic colours include some of the most vivid, not to say lurid primaries available in any class of dyes, and these can be mixed freely one with another to give compound shades. They have a natural affinity for wool and silk but will not dye cotton without chemical assistance. In this sense they could be classed as mordant dyes.

Basic dyes can be applied from the dyebath or made up into printing colours. The fixation of printed material presents no special technical difficulty. The great defect in this class is that the colours have very poor fastness to light and to washing.

Acid dyes

These are the dyes for dyeing and printing on silk and wool. They are given this name because the process of dyeing requires the presence of an acid.

The colours are brilliant, and available in immense variety. Within limits they can be mixed together to give compound shades. They can be dyed on to the fabric from an acidified dyebath, or made up into a thickened paste for application by any of the printing processes. Fixation of the printed material can be done satisfactorily in an improvised steamer.

The family is very large and diverse, and there is a corresponding inequality in the properties of individual colours. Care should be taken to choose only those with good fastness to light and to washing. There is plenty of choice.

Reactive dyes

This is an entirely new class of dyes, discovered in the I.C.I. laboratories and introduced by them in 1956 under the trade name Procion. Members of this class react chemically with the fibre being treated.

These dyes are soluble in water, and are suitable for application to the cellulosic fibres, to natural silk, or to chlorinated wool. They can be applied to the material from a dyebath, or made up into a thickened printing colour. Fixation of the printed material can be managed in several ways without special apparatus. The colours are outstandingly brilliant and have good fastness to light. Some of the colours have a tendency to 'bleed' if the wash is not very thoroughly done.

Mineral colours

Under this heading may be gathered a tiny class of colours formed in the fibre as precipitates from metallic salts. They are used mainly on the cellulosic fibres, and in the past played an important part in the calico printing industry. They can be applied by dyeing or by printing, and the fixation of printed material can be done without difficulty at home. The range of colours is seriously limited, but all have excellent fastness properties. The mineral colours have lost their once important position in industry, but the hand printer still finds them useful.

Occasional reference has been made throughout this chapter to the properties of fastness to light and to washing. These properties are inherent in the dye, and can be measured by

13

tests. There is now a series of internationally agreed standard tests for evaluating the fastness of a dye. The findings of the tests are represented by a number on a scale. The scale relating to light-fastness ranges from 1 to 8, in which the figure 8 stands for the highest fastness and the figure 1 the lowest. Other standard tests are designed to measure fastness to hot water and washing, to perspiration, and to the various cleaning and proofing chemicals. The findings of these other tests are represented on a scale ranging from 1 to 5, in which the figure 5 stands for the highest degree of fastness and the figure 1 the lowest. The manufacturers publish the fastness figures for all their dyestuffs.

It is not necessary for the amateur to understand the chemical constitution of his dyes; what he must understand is how to apply them. The art is to find and concentrate on those modes of application that can be made to succeed within the existing limitations of skill, time and equipment. In a general way, the dyer and printer gradually gets to understand his dyes much as the woodworker gets to know the behaviour of the various timbers.

3 · Hot dyeing

In the course of his work there are two situations where the craftsman will need to know how to dye a piece of fabric. The first is where the fabric is dyed to give it an all-over colour before being printed with some pattern. The second occurs in all the resist styles, such as tie-dye and batik, where dyeing comes at the end of the process. Dyeings of the first sort are usually done in a hot dyebath, those of the second are most often cold. This is no more than a rough workshop distinction, but it will be convenient to follow it for the moment in order to bring out certain differences in procedure.

A typical hot dyebath consists of a very small quantity of dyestuff dissolved in a very large quantity of water. The water distributes the dye evenly throughout the fabric being dyed. Fixation of the dye in the fabric takes place if the dyebath is brought to boiling point and kept there for about an hour. The uptake of the dye is a progressive action, rapid at first and getting gradually slower until an equilibrium is reached. Beyond this point the fabric will accept no more dye.

The depth of tone, or 'shade', of a piece of dyeing is determined by the concentration of dyestuff in the fabric. If we use 5 grams of dyestuff to dye a piece of material weighing 100 grams, this is a concentration of 5 in 100. In the jargon of the industry this would be known as a five per cent shade. Strengths of dyeings are invariably defined as percentages in this way.

The dyer can work out in advance how much dyestuff to put in his dyebath to dye any piece of fabric to any desired shade, as follows:

14

$$\frac{\text{weight of fabric} \times \text{X}}{100} = \text{weight of dyestuff}$$

where X is the desired shade expressed as a percentage.

If, for example, the dyer proposes to dye a piece of fabric weighing 238 grams with a five per cent shade of a given dyestuff:

$$\frac{238 \times 5}{100} = \frac{238}{20} = 11 \cdot 9 \text{ grams}$$

11·9 grams is the weight of dyestuff required.

This formula applies to all dyestuffs on all fabrics, whether they be weighed in grams or ounces. The arithmetic is easier if the weighing is done in grams. Those who find it more practical to weigh fabric in ounces should multiply the fabric weight by 28·35 to determine the weight in grams.

One question has not been answered: how does the dyer know what a five per cent shade looks like? To put it the other way round: how can he give a percentage figure to some shade which exists only in his mind's eye? The answer is that he can do neither without consulting a pattern.

Percentage figures of dye shades have no absolute value as, for instance, units of candle power. They can do no more than describe the concentration of a particular dye in a particular fabric. To know what a particular shade looks like on a particular fabric, the dyer must have in his hand a piece of that fabric dyed to that shade. In fact his most priceless reference book will be his pattern book. In this will be kept actual samples of all the fabrics he has dyed, with a written record of the dye concentration and any other item of technical

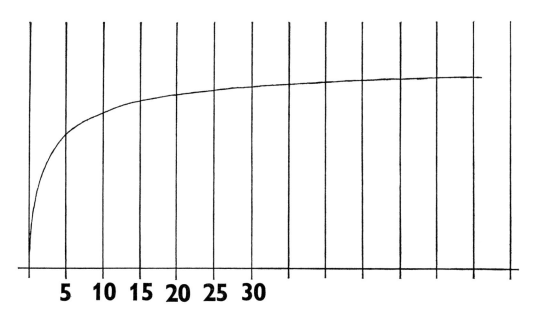

5 10 15 20 25 30

TIME IN MINUTES

FIG I   Rate-of-dyeing curve

significance. It is not possible to buy such a book, and without one the dyer is dependent on guesswork. The beginner should start his own pattern book with his first piece of dyeing.

It so happens that the concentration known as a five per cent shade is a useful general-purpose strength for dyeing, say, direct dyes on cotton, or acid dyes on wool. Paler shades are made by reducing the weight of dyestuff according to a diminishing geometric progression, thus:

$$\div 2, \div 4, \div 8, \div 16, \div 32, \div 64 \ldots$$

These steps will appear to be evenly spaced, and the dilution $\div 16$ is about half-way towards white. These smaller fractions cannot be weighed accurately without a fine balance. In such cases the amateur must improvise. A pair of kitchen scales will weigh down to five per cent of quite a small piece of fabric. This amount of dye powder should be tipped out on to a flat sheet of clean paper, and scraped together into a neat rectangular pile with a stainless steel knife. With care this pile can be cut in half, then into quarters, into eighths and so on. The method is more accurate than it sounds.

The dry dyestuff is now mixed with a little cold water, grinding it against the side of a pudding basin with the back of a stainless steel spoon until it becomes a perfectly smooth, creamy paste. Boiling water is then poured into this paste until all the dye is dissolved. This concentrated solution will later be stirred into the dyebath.

The most important piece of equipment in the dye shop is the container in which the dyeing will be done. This should be as big as possible, as good, level dyeing needs plenty of room. Stainless steel is the best material. Although expensive to buy, a stainless steel container will outlast many made of enamelled or galvanized iron, and will be much easier to keep clean. Suitable deep, seamless bowls are made for the dairy and catering trades. First attempts can be made in any available large pan in the kitchen.

A gas ring or gas burner is the most convenient form of heating because the heat can be controlled exactly and immediately. If a new installation is being made, the gas ring or burner should be of the heavy-duty type, and should be set about eighteen inches above floor level. This is to reduce the strain of lifting, and also to give the dyer a better view of what is happening inside. The dyer will also need a stout wooden stirring stick, strong enough to lift the whole weight of the wet material. He may like to wear a waterproof apron and rubber gloves.

The weight of the fabric being dyed decides the amount of dye solution (or liquor) needed in the dyebath. A ratio of thirty parts dye liquor to one part fabric is usual. In the present example the fabric weighed 238 grams. The dye liquor should therefore weigh $238 \times 30 = 7,140$ grams. This 30 : 1 ratio need not be measured with scrupulous accuracy, and for the present purpose it would be near enough to read 7,140 grams as 7,140 ccs, or a little over 7 litres (237 ozs).

It is important to understand that the strength or depth of shade is controlled by the weight of dyestuff concentrated in the fabric. It is not controlled by the amount of water put in the dyebath. If we add more water to the dyebath it will not make the dye paler. All that will happen will be a slowing down of the dyeing process; it will take longer to reach the point of equilibrium or saturation. A five per cent shade will always be a five per cent shade, whether the liquor-to-fabric ratio be 10:1, 20:1, 30:1 or 40:1. The recom-

16

PLATE I Cake tin steamer in action

PLATE 2 Curtains printed from children's blocks
Iron liquor on galled cotton

18

PLATE 3 Curtains printed from lino blocks cut by George and
    Margaret Bruce after Yoruba (Nigeria) designs
    Iron liquor on galled cotton

PLATE 4 Random printing with two very small wood blocks
Iron liquor on galled cotton

PLATE 5 Two-colour print from lino blocks by Cynthia Collins, aged 14
Direct dyes on cotton

PLATE 6 Lino block cut by Phyllis Barron

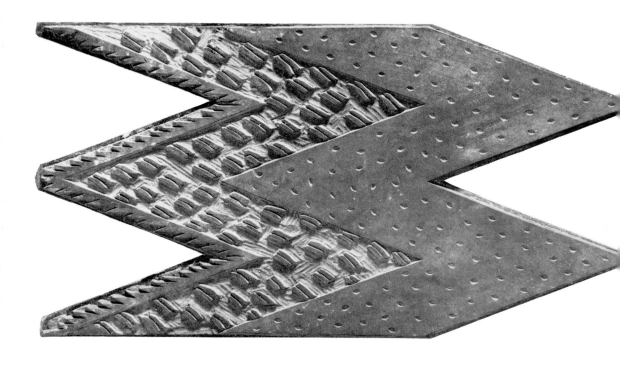

PLATE 7 Print from the block opposite. Iron liquor on galled linen

PLATE 8 French wood block print, mid 18th century
Madder and various mordants on cotton

Victoria and Albert Museum: Crown copyright reserved

24

mended ratio 30 : 1 is designed to ensure that there is ample room for the fabric to be turned in the dyebath. When the fabric is cramped for space it is almost impossible to avoid patchy and uneven dyeing. There are three golden rules for level dyeing: have plenty of dye liquor, keep the fabric moving, and dye slowly.

All water used for all dyeing purposes should, ideally, be distilled, but this is a counsel of perfection. Rain water makes a very good substitute. Hard water must be treated and softened artificially. If there is no water-softening installation, the batch of water for each occasion can be softened by stirring in a little sodium hexametaphosphate. This is sold under the trade name Calgon.

The dyebath is made ready by stirring the concentrated dye solution into sufficient water to make a total liquor-to-fabric ratio of 30 : 1. The temperature is then raised to between 30–40°C (85–105°F), which is about the temperature of a bath. While this is happening the fabric is wetted thoroughly by soaking it in water; hot water if possible. This helps the rapid diffusion of the dye when the fabric is first entered into the dyebath. The fabric is entered into the dyebath with the help of the wooden stick, which is used to keep it as spread out as possible and to open all tight folds and ropes. When the fabric is in, the gas is turned up, and the dyebath brought to the boil.

A glance at the rate-of-dyeing curve in fig 1 will show that the uptake of dye is at its most energetic during the first quarter of an hour. It is essential that the dyer should stand over his dyebath for the whole of this period to keep the fabric moving. After the first quarter of an hour the fabric should be stirred occasionally, the more often the better. The stirring stick should be worked about this way and that: if it is simply stirred round and round it will wind up the fabric on to itself. When boiling point has been reached common salt or Glauber's salt is usually added to the dyebath. The amount to add is roughly twice the weight of the dry dyestuff in solution. The salt should be added, a little at a time, at intervals spread over about half an hour. As dyeing proceeds, the dyebath will lose water by evaporation, and this loss must be made good by additions of boiling water. Before any addition or alteration is made to a dyebath (this or any other) the fabric must be temporarily lifted out.

Dyeing is complete in one hour from the time when the dyebath reached boiling point. The gas is then turned off, the remaining dye liquor thrown away, and the dyed fabric given a thorough rinse in running water. It may sound wasteful to throw away the remaining dye; there may still be some strength left in it. The trouble is that there is no way of knowing how much strength. What is certain is that a second piece of fabric dyed in the remaining dye liquor will come out paler than the first. Even worse, the dyer will have no control over the shade. The amateur should always make up a fresh dyebath for each job.

The procedure described in the foregoing paragraphs covers the ordinary application of direct dyes to cellulosic fibres by the hot dyebath. It applies equally to all other hot dyebaths with very little modification of detail, as follows:

DIRECT DYES ON SILK

As for cotton, except that Glauber's salt should be avoided because of its tendency to reduce the lustre. Boiling water has the same tendency, and so the dyebath should be kept just under the boil.

DIRECT DYES ON WOOL

As for cotton. A small amount (1%) of acetic acid may be added to the dyebath at the beginning and again towards the end of dyeing. Vigorous stirring may cause the wool to felt.

ACID DYES ON WOOL

Make up the dyebath with dyestuff, Glauber's salt, and sulphuric acid. The quantity of Glauber's salt and acid depends on the weight of dyestuff.

For a 5% shade the quantities would be:

dyestuff	5%
Glauber's salt	20%
sulphuric acid	5%

For an 0·5% shade the quantities would be:

dyestuff	0·5%
Glauber's salt	10%
Sulphuric acid	1%

The dyeing procedure is as for direct dyes. Vigorous stirring may cause the wool to felt. The percentage figures are in all cases percentages of the weight of fabric being dyed.

4 · Cold dyeing

The cold dyes come into their own in tie-dyeing and batik work. They make an odd assortment of old and new, natural products, metallic salts, and coal-tar derivatives. It is not possible to choose one as a model for the rest, as was done in the case of the hot dyes. They must be described one by one.

Indigo

Indigo is the oldest and still the most magnificent cold dye. It is applied to cellulosic fibres from a vat by a special procedure of repeated immersions. At each immersion the fabric takes up a little more dye, and in this way it is possible to control a progression of shades from pale to dark. All the shades of indigo are an attractive blue, and the deepest of all has an intense velvety richness over which lies an almost metallic haze resembling bronze.

Indigo dyeing begins with the making of a vat. For this the container should be deep rather than wide: a dustbin or garbage can serves very well. In this the indigo is converted into its unstable, reduced, leuco form, and dissolved in a weak alkali. A small selection of recipes for indigo vats is given below. Natural indigo is no longer obtainable in England or the United States. Synthetic indigo is offered in several different chemical forms, including indigo paste and indigo grains. It is important that the recipes should not be confused one with another. The recipe for indigo paste must not be used on indigo grains, and vice versa.

Indigo
ZINC-LIME VAT

In this, nascent hydrogen is the reducing agent and lime-water the solvent. When zinc dust is mixed with milk of lime it dissolves, forming calcium zincate and liberating hydrogen.

1 lb	indigo paste
2 ozs	zinc dust
5 lbs	quicklime
6 galls (960 ozs*)	water

Work the indigo paste and zinc dust to a smooth cream with water.
Work the quicklime to a smooth cream with water.
Add the above ingredients to the vat liquor, and raise the temperature to about 55°C, (130°F)
Stir gently until reduction is complete, that is, until vat liquor and sediment have turned yellow. This may take half an hour.
Allow the vat to settle before dyeing.

Indigo
HYDROSULPHITE VAT

In this, sodium hydrosulphite is the reducing agent, caustic soda the solvent.

1 lb	indigo paste
6 ozs	common salt
1½ ozs	caustic soda
3 ozs	sodium hydrosulphite
6 galls (960 ozs)	water

Add the ingredients to the vat in the order given. Warm to about 45°C, (110°F) and stir gently until reduction is complete, that is, until vat liquor turns yellow. This may take a quarter of an hour. Allow contents to settle before dyeing.

It will have been noticed in the above recipes that gentle heat is needed to bring about the reduction of the indigo. Once the vat liquor and sediment have turned yellow the heat can be turned off. In a good warm summer (18°C, 65°F) there is no need for any artificial heat under an indigo vat: in the winter a low gas might be lit, just to take off the chill.

The technique of dyeing is the same for both tie-dyeing and batik.

Lower the fabric gently into the vat, and see that it is totally immersed. Do everything possible to avoid carrying down into the liquor pockets of air trapped in the folds of the fabric. Take care not to disturb the sediment at the bottom of the vat. The easiest way to do this is to support the fabric on some type of open frame or basket suspended from above. Leave the fabric in the vat for about fifteen minutes.

* American readers should note that imperial gallons (160 ounces), imperial quarts (40 ounces), and imperial pints (20 ounces) are used throughout this text.

On being lifted out, the fabric should at first appear a brilliant yellowish-green, but this will darken quickly through emerald and dark bottle green until at last indigo blue appears. The change in colour indicates the change in the chemical state of the indigo as it reverts from its unstable leuco form to its stable blue form. The change is brought about by the oxygen in the air.

Whilst it is out of the vat, the fabric should, if possible, be spread out horizontally. If it is hung up, the liquor will drain down to the bottom edge and cause a band of uneven dyeing. The best place is out of doors, on a lawn or drying ground shaded from direct sunlight. When the fabric has turned to an even blue all over, it is returned to the vat for a further immersion.

This alternation of immersions and exposures to the air is continued until the dyer is satisfied. Each immersion adds a little more depth to the shade: five immersions would be a fair number, but some dyers are willing to go up to twenty. The timing can be worked out roughly by allowing fifteen minutes in followed by fifteen minutes out, but it is better to be guided by the colour of the fabric than by any strict count of time.

The process ends by rinsing the dyed fabric very thoroughly in running cold water. Fabric dyed in the zinc-lime vat should, if possible, go through a souring bath. This is simply a bath of cold water to which has been added a very little hydrochloric acid. The effect is to remove the impurities that are deposited in this vat, and so to brighten the blue of the indigo. After a few minutes, the soured fabric is lifted out and given a final rinse.

The secret of success with all indigo vats is to maintain the liquor in a state of chemical reduction for as long as possible. Every time the fabric is immersed, and every time the vat is stirred violently, oxygen is taken down into the liquor, and the life of the vat is shortened. In the end the clear greenish-yellow will give place to a steely grey liquid in which hang solid specks of precipitated indigo. The vat is then dead. Before any attempt is made to revive it, the fabric must be lifted out.

To revive an indigo vat, stir in a very little of the alkali and about half that amount of the reducing agent. Raise the temperature to about $55°C$ ($130°F$) and stir gently. Leave for about an hour. This treatment cannot be repeated indefinitely, as an excess of reducing agent will destroy the vat, and strip the indigo from any fabric put into it.

The premature death of a vat can be avoided by using the so-called Stock Vat method of dyeing. The active ingredients are first mixed together in a small amount of water to give a very concentrated solution. This is called the Stock Vat. Dyeing is done in the usual deep container filled with lukewarm water in which has been dissolved a very small quantity of the reducing agent. This is called the dyeing vat.

Suppose the dyer has decided to give his piece of fabric five immersions. He begins by stirring one-fifth of the Stock Vat into the dyeing vat, and he then immerses his fabric in this very weak liquor for a quarter of an hour. At the end of this time he withdraws the fabric and spreads it out to oxidize in the ordinary way. Whilst the fabric is out, he pours the second fifth of the Stock Vat into the dyeing vat. In this way he continues to add the remainder of the Stock Vat, a fraction at a time, whenever the fabric is taken out to oxidize.

This is a good method because:

1 It is always best to dye indigo from a weak vat progressing towards a strong vat.

2 The small additions of Stock Vat help to restore the state of chemical reduction in the dyeing vat each time the fabric is withdrawn.

STOCK VAT

1 lb	indigo grains
$4\frac{1}{2}$ ozs	caustic soda
$2\frac{1}{2}$ ozs	sodium hydrosulphite, all dissolved in
3 pints (60 ozs)	warm water, 50°C (120°F)

DYEING VAT

$\frac{1}{2}$ oz	sodium hydrosulphite
6 galls (960 ozs)	water

Anthraquinone vats

The anthraquinone vats offer a range of fast colours suitable for use with tie-dyeing and batik work on the cellulosic fibres. They are applied from a cold vat by an immersion-exposure sequence in some ways resembling the technique of indigo dyeing. The liquor-to-fabric ratio is usually kept short, say 20:1 or even shorter.

RECIPE TO DYE 100 GRAMS OF FABRIC

For larger pieces of fabric the quantities must be increased in proportion.

Dilute

40 grams	dyestuff paste, in
400 ccs (14 ozs)	soft water

Heat to 60°C (140°F), add

25 ccs	caustic soda solution in water (1:3 parts by weight)
10 grams	sodium hydrosulphite

Stir gently and leave for about 15 minutes whilst reduction takes place.

The reduced or leuco solution of the anthraquinone vats may be brown or violet, blue or green. The colour varies from dye to dye, but is usually darker than the parent colour.

Add to the reduced liquor

$1\frac{1}{2}$ litres (51 ozs)	cold soft water, in which has been dissolved
5 ccs	caustic soda solution in water (1:3 parts by weight)
2 grams	sodium hydrosulphite

Enter the fabric and work it about for 20 minutes, taking care not to drag air down into the liquor.

Withdraw the fabric and spread it out to oxidize.

Whilst the fabric is out, stir into the vat

10 grams	common salt

Return the fabric to the vat for a further twenty minutes. Withdraw the fabric for a second time and, whilst it is out, stir into the vat common salt as before. Three twenty-minute immersions should be sufficient. Some dyers prefer to give one immersion only, lasting for one hour.

When the fabric has been withdrawn and oxidized for the last time, it is given a thorough rinse in cold running water and then boiled in a solution of ordinary soap for fifteen minutes. This soap boiling is an important part of the fixation and development of all anthraquinone vat dyes.

Soluble vats

These offer the same range of colours as the parent vat dyes from which they are derived, and they have the same fastness properties. They are soluble in water and are applied from a cold dyebath, not a vat. The liquor-to-fabric ratio should be very short, say, 5:1. The final colour is formed in the fibre by oxidation in a developing bath.

RECIPE TO DYE 100 GRAMS OF FABRIC
For larger pieces of fabric the quantities must be increased in proportion.
    Dissolve
        5 grams   dyestuff, in
        500 ccs (17 ozs)   cold soft water
Enter the fabric and work it about for twenty minutes.
Lift the fabric out temporarily, and stir into the dyebath
        5 grams   Glauber's salt
Return the fabric to the dyebath for twenty minutes.
Lift the fabric out again and stir in as before
        5 grams   Glauber's salt
Return the fabric for a final twenty minutes.
Lift the impregnated material and plunge it into the first developing bath containing
        1 gram   sodium nitrite, dissolved in
        1 litre (34 ozs)   cold soft water
Work the fabric about for one minute and then plunge it into the second developing bath containing
        20 ccs   sulphuric acid, dissolved in
        1 litre (34 ozs)   cold soft water
Work the fabric about until the final colour is evenly developed: this should take only a few moments.
Dangerous nitrous fumes are given off by the second bath, and this part of the work must be done out of doors or by an open window.
To save space, the two baths may be combined in one. Dissolve 1 gram sodium nitrite in 2 litres (68 ozs) of cold water. Add 20 ccs sulphuric acid very carefully, drop by drop. Nitrous fumes are given off at once.
When the final colour is evenly developed, the fabric is given a thorough rinse in cold running water, and then boiled in a solution of ordinary soap for fifteen minutes. This soap boiling is an important part of the fixation and development of all soluble vat dyes.

Basic dyes

The basic dyes give colours of unequalled brilliance on cotton, wool and silk. They can be dyed cold, and are suitable for tie-dyeing. They are not suitable for wax-resist work because

30

they cannot withstand the final boiling treatment when the wax is cleared from the fabric.

To dissolve basic dyes, they must first be worked to a paste with about a third of their own volume of acetic acid. Boiling water is then poured into this paste, and stirring continued until a clear concentrated solution results.

To dye 100 grams of wool or silk, make a dyebath of 1 litre (34 ozs) of cold soft water and sharpen it with a very little acetic acid, say 1 cc. Dissolve 5 grams dyestuff in acetic acid and boiling water by the method given above. Stir one-third of this concentrated solution into the dyebath. Wet the fabric thoroughly in soft water, enter it and work it about in the liquor for twenty minutes. Lift the fabric temporarily and stir into the dyebath the second third of the concentrated solution. Return the fabric to the dyebath and work it about for another twenty minutes. At the end of this time lift the fabric, add the remaining third of the concentrated solution, and return the fabric for a final twenty minutes. If the style of work allows, there is no reason why this dyebath should not be heated gradually to about 82°C (180°F). At the end of the dyeing time, the fabric is given a thorough rinse in cold running water, washed in lukewarm water and rinsed again. It must never be boiled.

Basic dyes will not dye cotton unless the material has first been mordanted. The mordanting of tie-dye work should be done after the fabric has been tied up, not before.

TO MORDANT 100 GRAMS OF COTTON

Dissolve

| 10 grams | tannic acid powder, in |
| 500 ccs (17 ozs) | boiling water |

The tannic acid must be worked until all lumps are broken up and dissolved. The container and the stirring stick must be made of some non-ferrous material such as oven glassware, polythene (U.K.), polyethylene (U.S.A.), or wood.

The cotton fabric is immersed in the hot tannic acid solution and worked about with a stick until it is thoroughly well saturated and all air bubbles have risen to the top. It is then left overnight, sunk with stones if necessary so that no part rises out of the liquid. Next morning the fabric is lifted out, squeezed by hand, and plunged while still wet into a bath containing 5 grams tartar emetic dissolved in 500 ccs (17 ozs) water. It is worked about in this solution for half an hour and then lifted out, squeezed, and without delay entered into the dyebath.

TO DYE 100 GRAMS MORDANTED COTTON

Dissolve

| 5 grams | basic dyestuff |

in acetic acid and boiling water by the method given above.

Stir this solution into a dyebath consisting of

| 500 ccs (17 ozs) | cold soft water, sharpened with |
| 1 cc | acetic acid |

Enter the mordanted cotton and work it about in the dye liquor for half an hour.

Some dyers prefer to follow the method recommended for wool and silk. They divide their concentrated solution into three parts and add one part to the dyebath at ten-minute intervals. If the style of work allows, there is no reason why this dyebath should not be heated gradually. At the end of the dyeing time, the fabric is lifted out and washed as for wool.

Iron buff or rust

This is an ancient recipe for precipitating ferric oxide in the fibre by a simple chemical reaction. The colour is an attractive foxy brown, very fast to light and to boiling, but sensitive to acids. It is well known to housewives as the unwelcome iron spots that turn up on linen from time to time. Iron buff is suitable for tie-dying and batik work, and can be used in conjunction with indigo on the same piece of material.

Dissolve

1 lb	ferrous sulphate (copperas), in
1 gall (160 ozs)	hot water

Add to this solution

$\frac{1}{2}$ lb	lead acetate (poison)

Stir thoroughly and then leave for several hours, overnight if necessary.

At the end of this time a white precipitate will have settled to the bottom of the container. Above it will lie a clear green liquid: this is the rust liquor. Strain, or siphon off, the rust liquor into another container, without disturbing the sediment. Throw the sediment away: if it is not cleaned out at once, it will set hard and be almost impossible to remove.

Immerse the fabric in the cold rust liquor for one hour; lift it out to drain and dry.

Meanwhile prepare a developing bath containing

3 ozs	caustic soda, dissolved in
1 gall (160 ozs)	cold water

Immerse the rust-impregnated fabric in the developing bath for two minutes; lift it out to drain and dry.

The final colour change is produced gradually by the action of the oxygen in the air. When the change is complete, the fabric is given the usual thorough rinse in cold running water, a wash in hot water, and another rinse.

Reactive dyestuffs

These can be applied from a cold dyebath, and give a range of bright colours fast to light and to washing. Reactive dyes are sold as Procion (I.C.I.), Reactone (Geigy) and Cibacron (Ciba), among others. They are at their best on mercerized cotton, but may be used on unmercerized cotton, on linen and on viscose rayon. Because of their high reactivity with the fibre, they tend to penetrate the tied-up parts of tie-dye work. When used in batik they have the extra advantage that they can be converted at will into brown shades very like the traditional Javanese colours derived from the bark of the tingi, soga and tejeran trees. Procion dyes suitable for batik dyeing now all bear the prefix letter M-.

The Procion recipe which follows is typical of reactive dyes. Prepare a cold dyebath with a short liquor-to-fabric ratio as follows:

Dissolve

25 grams	urea, in
300 ccs (101·5 ozs)	boiling water

Leave to cool down to 60°C (140°F) and then add this solution slowly and carefully, stirring all the time to

    50 grams   Procion dyestuff

Finally add

    900 ccs (204 ozs)   cold water

In a separate container prepare an alkali solution as follows:

    4 grams   soda ash (anhydrous sodium carbonate)

    8 grams   sodium bicarbonate, dissolved in

    100 ccs (3·5 ozs)   cold water

Immediately before dyeing, stir the alkali solution into the Procion dyebath. Once the alkali has been added the dyebath is active for only two or three hours. Any liquor left at the end of this time must be thrown away, even though it looks the same as it did when fresh. Enter the fabric and work it about in the liquor for half an hour; lift it out to drain and dry.

Fixation takes place slowly if the dyed material is simply hung up in the air, say a night and a day, depending on the time of year and the conditions. In a warm, humid atmosphere the process is quicker, and in an improvised steamer it is complete in an hour. Instructions for making and using steamers will be given in a later chapter.

If desired, the bright primary colour may now be changed to a deep brown by immersing the dyed fabric in a short developing bath containing

    20 grams to every litre (34 ozs) of water   Brentamine Fast Black K Salt,
                                               I.C.I. (U.K.), or
                                             Fast Black K Salt (U.S.A.)

The colour change is almost instantaneous, and when it is evenly developed throughout, the fabric is ready to be washed.

The washing of all Procion dyeing and printing calls for great thoroughness. Begin by rinsing the material in cold running water until the water runs clear. Then rinse in warm water until the water runs clear. Then wash for a quarter of an hour in hot, not boiling, water to which has been added a little Lissapol (U.K.) or Synthrapol (U.S.A.). Finish with one more good rinse in cold running water.

5 · Thickening agents

A typical batch of textile printing colour is made up of two component parts: the active part which includes the dye, and an inactive part consisting of thickening matter. The thickening is added for two reasons: first to give body to the mixture so that it can be controlled during the printing process, and secondly to prevent the colour from spreading in the printed material by capillary attraction. A thickening agent should be soluble in water, chemically inert so that it will not react with the dye, and easily removable from the printed material during the wash-off.

The thickening agents in common use are all derived from vegetable starches and gums, the printer making up his own requirements to suit the job in hand. The block printer usually likes a sticky gum, the screen printer a free-flowing paste that will not clog his screen. The choice depends on the style of work, on the class of dyestuff being used, and on the kind of textile being printed.

Gum tragacanth

SOMETIMES KNOWN AS GUM DRAGON

Derived from the tree *Astragalus gummifer*, this gum is imported in the form of whitish or yellowish horny flakes. These will take up to twenty times their own weight of water, giving a paste with a low solid content. The preparation of tragacanth paste is tedious and requires overnight steeping followed by lengthy boiling with stirring.

Tragacanth is an excellent all-round thickening for almost any dye on cotton, silk or wool. It behaves well in screen printing, but is not by itself sticky enough for some kinds of block printing. It comes away readily in the wash-off.

Starch-Tragacanth

Laundry starch alone makes a sticky paste more suitable than tragacanth for block printing, but it is inclined to clog the mesh of the silk screen. Printing colour thickened with starch clings tenaciously to the printed material and is not easily removed in the wash-off.

By making a mixture of starch paste and gum tragacanth, the advantages of both are retained and the disadvantages reduced. The relative proportions may be varied at will.

British gum

British gum is manufactured by roasting starch under carefully controlled conditions. It makes a sticky paste with a high solid content, well suited to block printing. It can be used with most dyes for printing on cotton or silk. Colours thickened with British gum cling to the printed material, and the wash-off needs patience.

Gum senegal and gum arabic

Gums of this class come from various species of acacia tree growing in Africa, India and Australia. The best gum comes from Senegal, and is usually given that name. All types are imported as irregular, semi-transparent, yellowish nodules containing a greater or lesser amount of chaff and grit. When steeped in water, boiled and strained, they produce a sticky mucilage with a high solid content particularly suited to block printing. These gums should not be mixed with other thickenings.

Like British gum they can be used with most dyes; unlike British gum they dissolve readily and come away easily in the wash-off. They are the thickening preferred by printers on silk.

Sodium alginate

Sodium alginate thickening is manufactured from seaweed and sold as a straw-coloured powder under the trade name Manutex (U.K.) or Keltex (U.S.A.). It has many advantages.

Being a standardized product it has none of the variability sometimes found in natural gums, and it contains no impurity. The paste is made by simply stirring the powder into cold water; sieving is not necessary. Alginate thickening (Manutex or Keltex) can be used on all fibres and with all classes of dye except basic, chrome mordant, and recipes containing salts of heavy metals. It is the only thickening suitable for use with Procions (reactives). The texture of the paste can be adjusted to suit any style of printing. It has a very low solid content and is not sticky. Block printers who like a sticky paste can mix together Manutex or Keltex and British gum. Alginate thickenings come away readily in the wash-off.

When making up a batch of printing colour it is absolutely essential that the texture or working consistency should be just right. If it is too thick it will cake, if too thin it will run. The ideal consistency lies somewhere in between, and this has to be found by the printer. For several reasons it is not possible to define this consistency in a recipe. In the first place the natural gums are a somewhat variable raw material, and produce pastes of very different textures according to the length of time they have been boiled or left to stand. In the second place each printing process requires its own special texture. Adjustments have also to be made to suit the absorbency of the fabric being printed and the style of design, whether broad or fine. Any adjustment of texture must be made in the thickening part of the recipe; the active, or dye-containing part must not be tampered with. The beginner would be wise to learn as soon as possible how to make such adjustment, and the best way is by practical test on a spare piece of fabric.

Choose an easy recipe and prepare three lots of thickening, one as published, one too thick, one too thin. Make up three batches of colour using these thickenings, and try to print with them. Next make a run of intermediate mixtures between the batch as published and the too-thick batch, and between the batch as published and the too-thin batch. Print these alongside the first set of prints. A short time given to this exercise will soon show what feels right, and what gives the best prints.

As a very general guide, it is best to keep the paste as thin as can be managed without running. Pastes containing too much solid give trouble at a later stage. They are difficult to fix, difficult to wash off, give a poor colour yield in the printed areas, and tend to bleed into the unprinted areas. No serious piece of printing should ever be started unless the printer is satisfied with the working consistency of his colour. The only adjustment that should be needed once printing has started is a small addition of water to replace loss by evaporation.

Recipes for thickening

GUM TRAGACANTH

Soak 70 grams tragacanth flakes in 1 litre (34 ozs) of cold water (11 ozs gum in 160 ozs water).

Leave for two or three days, stirring occasionally.

Place in a double saucepan or porridge boiler and boil gently for eight hours, stirring and adding water from time to time to replace loss by evaporation.

Cool and strain.

STARCH-TRAGACANTH

Recipe for starch paste

20 parts by weight	laundry starch
200 parts by weight	cold water
10 parts by weight	olive oil

Work the starch to a smooth creamy paste with a little of the water.

Add the remainder of the water and then the olive oil, stirring all the time.

Boil gently and stir continuously until the starch thickens, and for a minute afterwards.

Turn off the gas, and stir the starch as it cools.

Starch paste is mixed with gum tragacanth prepared as in the foregoing paragraph.

The proportions of each might be anywhere between tragacanth 2 : starch 1, and tragacanth 1 : starch 1, according to the printer's judgment.

BRITISH GUM

For a stiff paste

50 parts by weight	British gum D
50 parts by weight	water

For a thinner paste

20 parts by weight	British gum D
80 parts by weight	water

In either case, add the whole of the British gum powder to the whole of the water; do not paste like starch.

Boil gently for half an hour, stirring all the time.

Leave to cool.

British gum thickens up considerably when it cools.

GUM ARABIC

Soak 600 grams gum arabic lumps in 1 litre (34 ozs) of cold water (6 lbs in 1 gall – 160 ozs).

Leave for several days, stirring occasionally.

Skim off the woody particles that have floated to the surface.

Boil the gum gently for three or four hours in a double saucepan, stirring frequently.

Pour the resulting liquid into a deep container and stand it aside for several days to allow the fine gritty particles to settle to the bottom.

The clear gum lying above the grit is then carefully poured off through a strainer.

SODIUM ALGINATE (Recipe using Manutex R.S., U.K.)

For a stiff paste

5 parts by weight	Manutex R.S.
100 parts by weight	cold water

For a thinner paste

2 parts by weight	Manutex R.S.
100 parts by weight	cold water

36

The flow characteristics of the paste can be adjusted by dissolving Calgon in the water. This must be done before the Manutex is added. For a 'short' paste with high viscosity, the Calgon should be five per cent of the weight of the Manutex. For a paste with a long flow, the Calgon might be twenty-five per cent of the weight of the Manutex. By varying the amounts of Calgon and Manutex, any desired consistency can be produced. For example:

Block printing consistency

1 gram	Calgon
20 grams	Manutex R.S.
1 litre (34 ozs)	cold water

Screen printing consistency

12·5 grams	Calgon
50 grams	Manutex R.S.
1 litre (34 ozs)	cold water

The method of preparing the paste is always the same, whatever the proportions of the ingredients.

1 Dissolve the Calgon in a little of the water which for this purpose may be warmed, if necessary, to about 60°C (140°F).
2 Add the remainder of the cold water.
3 Stir the Calgon solution briskly, and pour in the Manutex powder as a steady stream or drift. Continue stirring until the Manutex particles have swollen and formed a thick suspension (five to ten minutes).
4 Leave to stand for a further twenty minutes during which time the paste will assume a clear, uniform, glassy texture.
5 Give a final short stir just before use.

Manutex and Keltex thickening, and printing colours made with Manutex or Keltex, must not be boiled.

SODIUM ALGINATE (Recipe using Keltex, U.S.A.)

To make a five per cent stock paste for screen printing (128 ozs):

102 ozs	cold water
0·62 cc	preservative (Dowicide A)
0·41 cc	ammonia 28%
127 grams	Improved Keltex S

Stock paste is thinned or thickened with additional water or additional thickener after adding dyestuff, according to dyestuff manufacturers' instructions. A five per cent stock paste will require considerable thinning for block printing.

1 Add preservative and ammonia to water.
2 Under high-speed agitation, quickly sprinkle Keltex into solution.
3 After thirty minutes of mixing, paste is ready for use.

6 · Printing colours

Textile printing is sometimes called pattern dyeing or local dyeing, and these are good names because they describe what takes place. The printer applies his colour by one of the printing processes and fixes it in the fabric as a dye. The unprinted areas remain undyed, and when the fabric is washed the dye does not, or should not, migrate from the dyed to the undyed areas. It is very much more difficult to manage this local fixation than it is to dye the whole piece by immersion.

Most primitive cultures have a love of surface decoration and, as would be expected, this is well displayed in their fabrics. We find patterns produced on the loom by interweaving different coloured yarns, we find all kinds of decoration applied to the surface by needle-work, and we find painted and stencilled and block-printed patterns done in pigment pastes

FIG 2   Print from leaf stencil, Fiji

and vegetable stains, but we do not find dye printing. If we find pattern dyeing at all, we find it as one of the so-called resist styles, tie-dyeing or batik, and in both of these the dye is applied by immersing the whole piece in the dye bath.

The ability to apply dyes by printing calls for a combination of chemical and technical control beyond the scope of primitive man. Indeed, dye printing has been one of the slowest crafts to develop, emerging from a state of twilight only in the mid-nineteenth century. We can now see that the reason for this late development was the obscure and elusive nature of the dyes themselves; until they were understood the craft could only mark time.

The mechanism of dye printing is essentially simple: two or more substances are applied to the fabric, and the conditions so adjusted that they will react together in the presence of the fibre. The product of the reaction is the dye, the stable, insoluble colour intimately associated with the fibre in which it has been formed. This process can be demonstrated in an example.

The mordant dyes are insoluble colour lakes precipitated in the fibre by the reaction between the parent colour and the mordant. This can be done in three possible ways:

1 The pattern can be printed in a thickened solution of the mordant, and the fabric then boiled in a solution of the parent colour. Where colour meets mordant in the printed areas, an insoluble precipitate is formed in the fibre. In the unprinted areas no precipitate is formed, the colour remains soluble, and in due course comes away in the wash, leaving the fabric white.

This method is usually called the dyed style, and is particularly associated with madder. It has been known for at least two thousand years, but is today supplanted in industrial societies by quicker and more direct methods.

2 The whole of the fabric can be impregnated by immersing it in a solution of the mordant, and when this is dry the pattern can be printed in a thickened solution of the parent colour. Here again, where colour meets mordant a precipitate will be formed, whilst elsewhere the fabric remains white.

This method and the one above are not altogether satisfactory for two reasons: in each of them one of the active ingredients, mordant or colour, is dispersed throughout the whole of the fabric. This is not only wasteful of materials, it may be and often is the direct cause of a stained background. The ideal arrangement would be to confine both parent colour and mordant to the printed area, and to leave the remainder of the fabric empty.

3 This is the modern, and best version of mordant dye printing. The printing paste consists of a thickened mixture of colour and mordant. Under ordinary atmospheric conditions this mixture is reasonably stable and the ingredients will not react spontaneously. When the printing is finished and dry, the printer initiates the reaction by exposing the material to an atmosphere of steam. At the end of the steaming, the chemical reaction should be complete. This means that the ingredients should have assumed their final stable and insoluble form. When the material is washed, the excess colour deposited in the act of printing will come away in the water. For an anxious moment the printer will see his white material immersed in water strongly coloured with the surplus dye as it drains out of the printed areas. But this colour in the water is not active as a dye; it consists of fine solid particles of insoluble colour. As the rinsing is continued, the water will slowly clear until at last the material emerges perfectly white, except in the printed areas.

The foregoing account of the application of mordant colours illustrates the general procedure in dye printing. The different dye families require different ingredients in the printing paste, and there are differences in the method of fixation or development. Some dyes are fixed by passing the printed material through a chemical solution, but by far the greater number are fixed by steam. The construction and handling of steamers will be discussed in a later chapter.

To make up a batch of printing paste the printer need not be a chemist, but he must set about the work as if he were a chemist. He will need a set of weights and graduated measures, and he will need to be able to make simple calculations. The calculations will be that much simpler if he does his measurements in grams and litres. It is not safe, or even possible, to go by appearances. A batch of printing paste may have something like the colour of the dye intended, it may be almost colourless, or it may have some quite arbitrary colour that will be changed to the true colour during the development or fixation.

From the very beginning the printer should keep a written record of all his work: a workshop notebook in which are preserved actual pieces of printed and dyed material, each example supported by a detailed technical explanation. This should give all the information necessary to repeat the colour shown in the example, and should be written in ink in a legible hand.

The printing colour should be made up fresh for each job, and it is better to make up too much than too little. Working as the amateur does in quantities around a pint or a litre, a small human error in measuring some of the smaller ingredients leads to a disproportionately large difference in the final colour. If the printing colour runs out half-way through the work, it is almost impossible to make a perfect match. As a very rough guide to quantity, a pint (20 ozs) of colour will print about three yards of material. If the printing covers more than half the surface area, more will be required; if less, less. In any case something extra must be allowed for preliminary trial prints.

The ingredients should be set out on the work bench, together with the necessary scales, weights, measures, containers and stirring implements. Close at hand should be a gas ring or gas burner, and a sink with running water. The recipe should be copied out on to a separate sheet of paper. If the recipe book is put down on the bench, sooner or later somebody will spill something on it.

There should be no more difficulty in following a printing colour recipe than in following a recipe in a cookery book; the procedure is the same. Beginning at the top, the ingredients are measured out in the order given, and carefully ground, sieved, or mixed exactly in the way described. Where the recipe says 'leave until cold', this instruction must be scrupulously obeyed: carelessness at this point may precipitate the insoluble colour in the mixing bowl, and if this happens the paste is useless.

In the chapter on dyeing it was explained that the depth of shade is usually expressed as a percentage, the figure standing for the concentration of dyestuff in the fabric being dyed. For example, if we dye a piece of fabric weighing 100 grams in a dyebath containing 4 grams of dye, we say that we have dyed that fabric to a four per cent shade. In measuring the strength of printing colours, the percentage sign is used again, but with a quite different meaning. The beginner must beware of confusion. In printing colours the percentage figure stands for the concentration of dye in the paste. For example, if the total weight of a batch

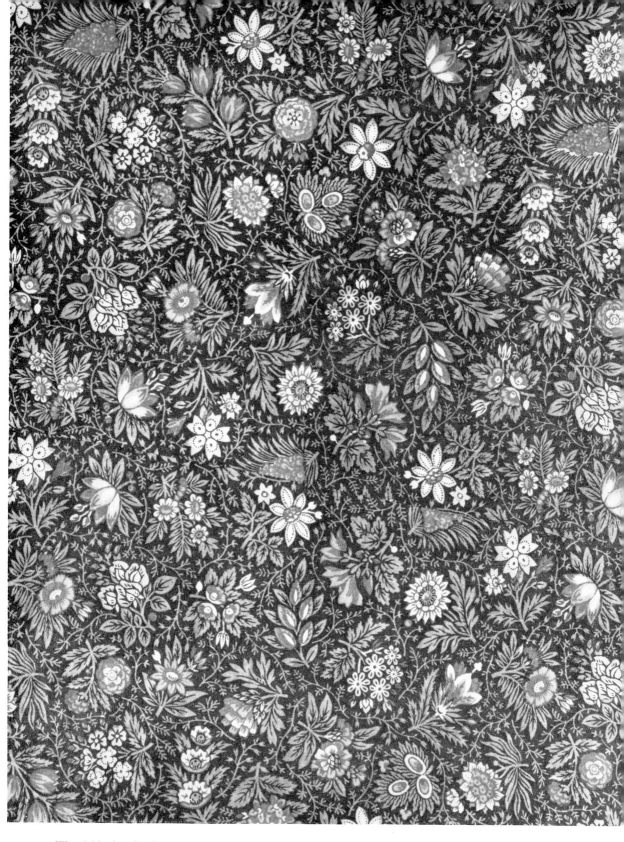

PLATE 9 Wood block print in the 'Rameneur' style
Provence, mid 19th century
Indigo, madder and other vegetable dyes on cotton

41

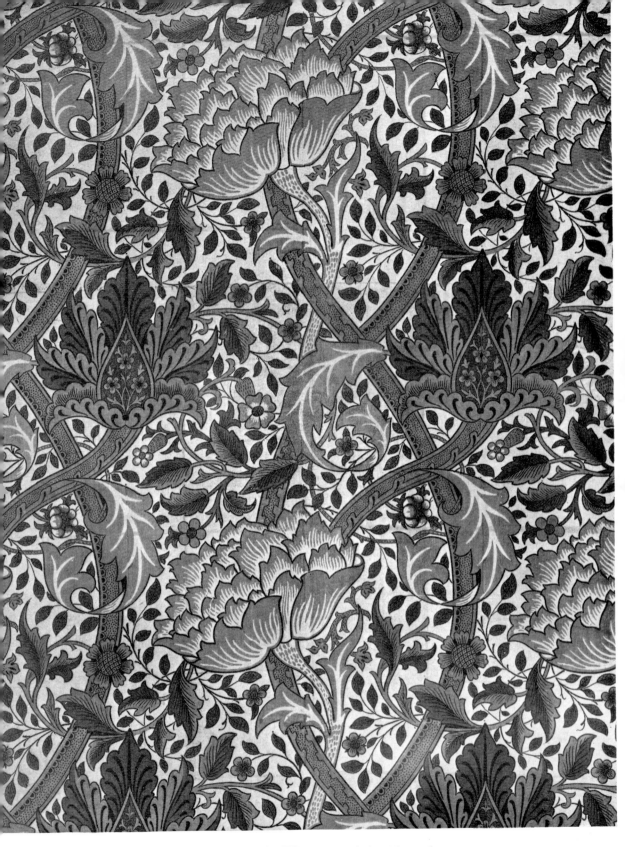

PLATE 10 'Windrush', designed by William Morris in 1883, and
block printed on cotton in the Morris workshops

PLATE 11 Amateur block printer at work

PLATE 12 Screen print by Ian Logan
Pigment colour on grey flannel

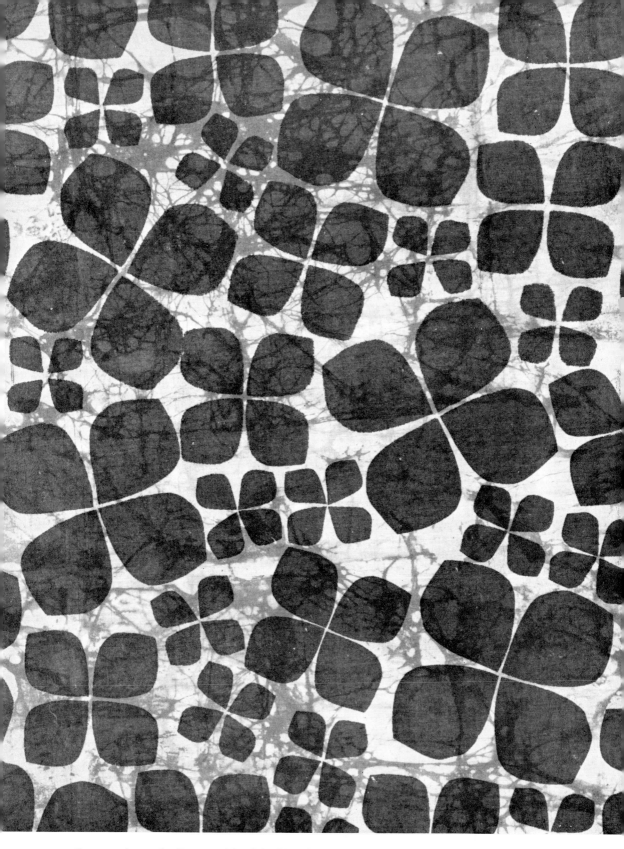

PLATE 13 Screen print on batik ground by Ada Cherniak

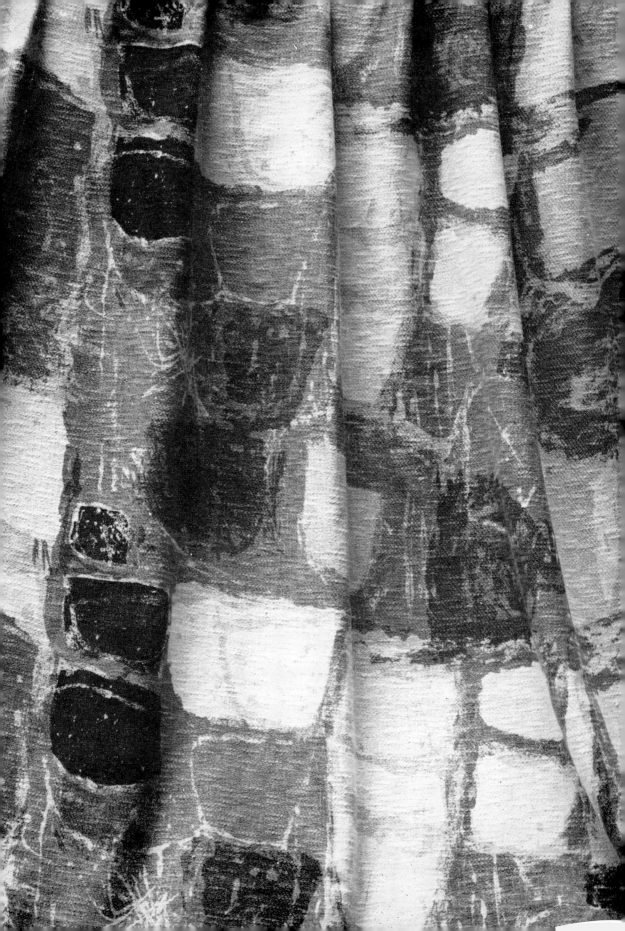

PLATE 15 'Summer Flowers' designed by Ivon and John Hitchens
Screen printed on heavy cotton by Hull Traders Ltd

PLATE 16 Tie-dyed curtains
Indigo vat on unbleached cotton

PLATE 17 Wall hanging (detail)
Screen printing, tin printing, freehand painting
Pigment colours on heavy cotton
Designed and printed by a group of spastic children
after a visit to Coventry Cathedral

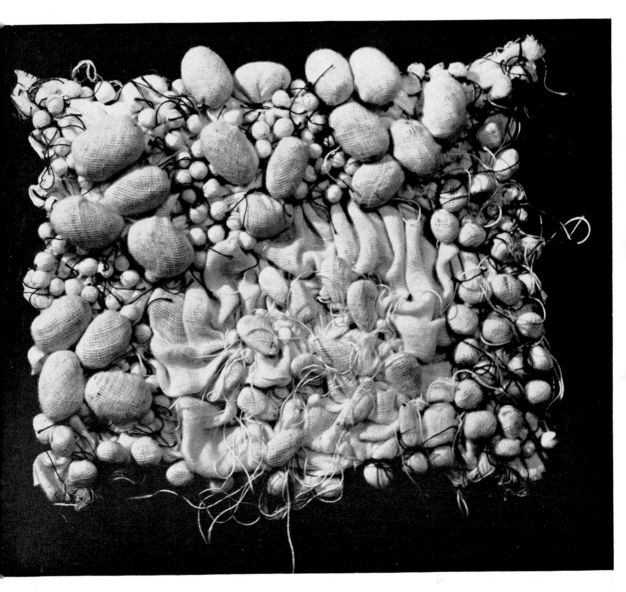

PLATE 18 Cotton muslin tied up ready for dyeing

PLATE 19 Tie-dyeing Yoruba (Nigeria), mid 20th century
Indigo vat on cotton

PLATE 20 Batik shoulder cloth (Slendang)
Java Tjirebon (?), 19th century
Vegetable dyes on cotton

PLATE 21 Batik sarong (detail)
Java Djakarta (?), mid 20th century
Synthetic dyes on cotton

53

PLATE 22 'Warrior'. Detail of hanging by Sheila Wright
Wax resist and 'Indigosol' dyes on natural silk

54

PLATE 23 Freehand painting
Yoruba (Nigeria), mid 20th century
Cassava paste resist, indigo vat on cotton

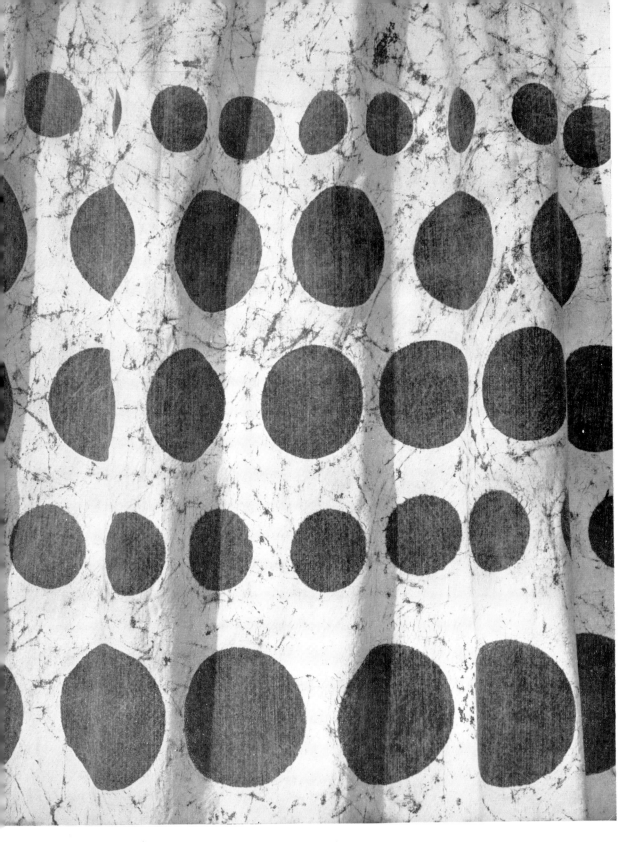

PLATE 24 Stencil decoration in flour paste resist
Dye applied by brush

of printing colour is 100 grams, and contained in it are 4 grams of dye, this batch of colour would be said to have a strength of four per cent. Most of the remaining ninety-six per cent would be taken up by the gum thickening.

In those cases where the same dye can be used both for dyeing and for printing, it must be clearly understood that there is no simple correspondence between the percentage figure for dyeing and the percentage figure for printing with that dye. The shade produced by dyeing at a concentration of four per cent is not necessarily equivalent to the shade produced by printing with a four per cent paste of the same dye. It so happens that a four per cent printing colour would be a pretty strong mixture. It is difficult to speak with any accuracy of a 'full strength' mixture, but in conversation this is often done. To save space, the recipe books usually publish only the 'full strength' recipe of a printing colour: the printer is left to make paler shades for himself. This is done by diluting the full strength colour in what is called reduction paste, a batch of thickening made up to the same consistency as the printing paste, but without colour.

It is impossible to estimate the strength of a reduced colour by looking at the contents of the mixing bowl: the ingredients must be measured. Fortunately for the amateur, the strength of paler shades can be controlled by following a very simple rule. To produce on the fabric a series of shades of the same colour gradating from dark to light through what appear to be evenly spaced steps, the printer must reduce by half at each step the amount of printing colour added to the reduction paste.

The beginner would do well to go through this exercise with all his colours, and to preserve the printed examples in his pattern book.

		'FULL STRENGTH' PRINTING COLOUR	REDUCTION PASTE
1	Darkest shade	1 pint	none
2	Paler	$\frac{1}{2}$ pint	$\frac{1}{2}$ pint
3	Paler	$\frac{1}{4}$ pint	$\frac{3}{4}$ pint
4	Paler	$\frac{1}{8}$ pint	$\frac{7}{8}$ pint
5	Paler	$\frac{1}{16}$ pint	$\frac{15}{16}$ pint

and so on . . .

Intermediate shades can be produced by subdividing the quantities still further according to the same geometric principle. Mixtures of two or more colours must also be controlled by measurement. For example, the beginner who is trying to get a particular green will find his quickest way to it if he undertakes the following exercise. The work may take half a morning to do, but if he preserves the examples he will never need to do it again.

	BLUE PRINTING COLOUR	YELLOW PRINTING COLOUR
Blue-green	$\frac{7}{8}$ pint	$\frac{1}{8}$ pint
	$\frac{3}{4}$ pint	$\frac{1}{4}$ pint
	$\frac{1}{2}$ pint	$\frac{1}{2}$ pint
	$\frac{1}{4}$ pint	$\frac{3}{4}$ pint
Yellow-green	$\frac{1}{8}$ pint	$\frac{7}{8}$ pint

It will be understood that all these tests on fabric must be given the full treatment. After printing, the dye must be fixed by steam or chemical developer according to the instructions in the recipe, and after fixing the material must be washed and ironed.

In the recipes which follow, it will be found that certain standard procedures occur time after time.

I THE DYESTUFF IS PASTED

Most dyestuffs are marketed as dry solids, and it is as dry solids that they must be weighed. After weighing, the dry dye powder is tipped into a mixing bowl, and a little cold water added, a few drops only, not too much. With the back of a stainless steel spoon or wooden spatula, the dye powder and water are ground to a smooth creamy paste against the side of the mixing bowl. Boiling water is then usually added, to bring the paste into solution. Any other solid ingredient that is reluctant to dissolve in cold water should be dealt with in the same way, having first been weighed in the dry state.

2 THE MIXTURE IS BOILED

For mixing small quantities, by far the most convenient container is a 'Pyrex' mixing bowl. The contents can be simmered by standing the bowl in a saucepan quarter full of boiling water on a gas ring or burner. At a later stage the contents can be cooled down by standing the bowl in cold running water.

Whenever thickening is mentioned in a printing recipe, what is meant is the thickening already made up to a consistency suitable for printing. Thus, 500 grams gum tragacanth in this context would mean not the dry solid flakes but the watery fluid prepared from them. It is best to make up all thickenings a bit too thick, because although it is easy to thin them down with water at the last minute, it is difficult, if not impossible, to make them thicker.

Some of the recipes are given in both metric and English measurements (with American equivalents in parentheses), set out side by side in vertical columns. This arrangement is for the convenience of printers who may prefer to work in one system rather than the other. But whichever he prefers, the printer must keep to that system right through the recipe: the quantities in one vertical column are not the same as those in the other column; for example, 1,000 grams is not the same as one gallon. In one or two cases, alternative versions are given. Printers often find that they get better results with one than with another. After all, dye printing is an art as much as a science. The ultimate authority on the reaction at the heart of the process is the chemist, but few chemists are printers. In practice, the printer gets along as well as he can with a combination of intuition, opportunism and experience.

FIG 3   Leaf stencil, Fiji

58

Recipes

DIRECT DYESTUFFS

for cotton, linen, silk, viscose rayon

In this recipe, the quantities in the two vertical columns are approximately equivalent.

Mix together

10 grams =	3 level teaspoons (U.K.)	dyestuff
33 grams =	14 level teaspoons (U.K.)	urea
80 ccs =	3 fluid ozs	warm water

Boil up together and stir until dissolved. Leave to cool.

When cool, add to sodium alginate thickening prepared as follows:

Dissolve

1 gram =	$\frac{1}{2}$ level teaspoon (U.K.)	Calgon, in
200 ccs =	7 fluid ozs	cold water

Stir this solution briskly with a fork, and pour in as a fine drift

Manutex R.S. (U.K.) or Keltex (U.S.A.)

to give a block printing consistency	4 grams = 1 level teaspoon (U.K.)
to give a screen printing consistency	7 grams = 2 level teaspoons (U.K.)

Continue stirring for five minutes and then leave for a further fifteen minutes to allow the paste to thicken.

Finally stir in

7 grams = 3 level teaspoons (U.K.)   disodium phosphate

Gum tragacanth may be used in the place of sodium alginate thickening, or, when printing on silk, gum arabic.

Leave the printed material to dry, and then steam for one hour.

Rinse thoroughly in cold running water.

Wash carefully in tepid water.

Fabrics printed with direct colours must never be boiled, as the dye is only loosely held.

CHROME MORDANT DYESTUFFS

for cotton, linen, viscose rayon

In this recipe the four vertical columns give four different strengths of the same colour, that on the right being the strongest.

Mix together

20	30	40	60 grams	dyestuff
320	280	240	160 ccs	hot water
(11)	(9·5)	(8)	(5·5 ozs)	
600	600	600	600 ccs	thickening
(20·5)	(20·5)	(20·5)	(20·5 ozs)	

Heat and stir until dissolved. Leave to cool.

When cold add

60	90	120	180 grams	chromium acetate liquor 32° Tw

Gum tragacanth, or starch-tragacanth mixtures, are the best thickening. Gum arabic and sodium alginate thickenings are not suitable.

The chromium acetate liquor must not be added until the mixture is cold. The figure 32° Tw is a measure of specific gravity on Twaddell's hydrometer: the liquor is sold in this form, ready for use.

Leave the printed material to dry, then steam for one hour.

Rinse thoroughly in cold running water.

Wash in hot water containing Teepol or Stergene (U.K.), Duponol or Synthrapol (U.S.A.). Rinse again in cold running water.

CHROME MORDANT COLOURS PRINTED AS EMULSIONS

In this new technique, the classical thickenings are replaced by an emulsion. There are several great advantages. The preparation of the emulsion is very much simpler than the preparation of tragacanth mixtures and, once made, it will keep for months without deterioration. Printing colours made with emulsion flow well during printing and do not clog. Fixation in the steamer is quicker and more complete, and the washing of the fabric easier than with colours made with tragacanth.

The most obvious advantage of emulsion printing is in the improved brightness of colour and softness of handle in the finished material. With this new technique, using one recipe only, the amateur can print a full palette of good, fast colours on cotton, linen, viscose rayon, natural silk, chlorinated wool, or any mixture of these fibres.

Preparation of emulsion

Dissolve

15 grams	Emulose B (D & H), in
210 ccs (7 ozs)	hot water, then stir in
75 grams	Glydote B (I.C.I.) or Kromofax (U.S.A.)

Stir briskly for a few seconds and let stand overnight.

Next morning stir the solution slowly and add little by little

700 ccs (24 ozs)   paraffin (kerosene)

Continue stirring until a homogeneous creamy emulsion is produced.

Then whisk the emulsion for a few minutes in a high-speed kitchen mixer, or with a mixer attached to an electric drill. It is then ready for immediate use, or can be kept in a screw-topped jar.

(Although designed for use with chrome mordant colours, this emulsion can be used with Direct colours and with Fast Black.)

Printing paste with emulsion: the five vertical columns give five different strengths of the same colour.

Mix together

20	30	40	50	60 grams	dyestuff
50	50	50	50	50 grams	urea
270	230	190	150	110 ccs	hot water
(9)	(8)	(6·5)	(5)	(4 ozs)	

Heat until dissolved.

Leave to cool.

When cold add

| 60 | 90 | 120 | 150 | 180 grams | chromium acetate 32° Tw |

Then stir the mixture into

| 600 | 600 | 600 | 600 | 600 grams | emulsion |

Reduction paste for use with the above recipe:

Dissolve

| 50 grams | urea, in |
| 225 ccs (7·5 ozs) | warm water |

Leave to cool.

When cold add

| 25 grams | chromium acetate 32° Tw |

Then stir the mixture into

| 700 grams | emulsion |

Leave the printed material to dry, steam for one hour or less, rinse and wash in the usual way.

YOUNG'S FAST BLACK

for cotton and linen

    Mix together cold

| 1 part by volume | Fast Black |
| 4 parts by volume | thickening |

A few drops of acetic acid (40%) should be added to the thickening before stirring in the Fast Black.

Tragacanth and starch mixtures are suitable, gum arabic and sodium alginate thickenings are not suitable.

Leave the printed material to dry, then steam for one hour.

Rinse in cold water, wash in hot water, rinse again.

This is one of the very few vegetable dyes still in use in printing. The colour contains Logwood extract and a mordant.

STEAM MANGANESE BROWN

for cotton and linen

This recipe should be made up fresh before use.

    Mix together

| 20 grams | sodium or potassium dichromate (poison) |
| 120 grams | thickening |

Boil up and stir until dissolved.

Leave to cool

When cold add

| 25 grams | manganese chloride |
| 25 grams | sodium acetate solution 1:4, i.e., 5 grams sodium acetate in 20 grams water |

Leave the printed material to dry.

The reaction will take place by simple exposure to the air, but one hour in the steamer gives better fixation.

Rinse in cold water, wash in hot water, rinse again.

This is an old mineral salt recipe giving a deep sepia colour, absolutely fast to light and to washing.

IRON BUFF (RUST)
for cotton and linen
Required:

> 1 glass or earthenware jar to hold 2 quarts (80 ozs)
> 1 lb green copperas (ferrous sulphate)
> 1 quart (40 ozs) hot water
> $\frac{1}{2}$ lb lead acetate (poison)

Put the copperas into the jar, and add the hot water. Stir with a wooden stick until dissolved.

Add the lead acetate, and stir again.

Cover the jar tightly and leave for at least two hours for the contents to settle.

Pour off the clear green liquid without disturbing the sediment. The green liquid is stock Rust Liquor; it will keep in a tightly stoppered bottle.

The white sediment must be washed away at once, or it will set hard in the container. Print with equal quantities of Rust Liquor and thickening, either tragacanth or British gum.

Leave the printed material until it is thoroughly dry, and then immerse it for two minutes in a two per cent solution of caustic soda (3 ounces of caustic soda dissolved in 1 gallon (160 ozs) cold water).

Lift out the impregnated material, and leave it to drain.

The reaction is completed by the action of atmospheric oxygen. Steaming is not necessary. When the colour is fully developed, the material is given the usual laundering, a thorough rinse in running cold water, a wash in hot water, and a final rinse in cold.

This is another old mineral salt recipe. The final colour – ferric oxide – is a beautiful foxy brown, absolutely fast to light and to washing.

IRON BLACK
for cotton and linen
The material must first be prepared by impregnating it with a solution of tannic acid. This is done in a gall bath, as follows:

> In a non-ferrous container dissolve

> 4 ozs   ground galls or tannic acid powder, in
> 2 galls (320 ozs)   hot water

First work the tannic acid powder to a smooth creamy paste with a little of the hot water, and then pour in the remaining hot water, stirring all the time.

Immerse the fabric in the gall bath, squeeze it once or twice to encourage penetration. Leave the fabric in the bath overnight, sinking it with stones if necessary so that no part rises out of the liquid.

62

Next morning lift the fabric, squeeze it, and spread it out to dry without washing. Whilst still damp it must not touch anything made of iron, or it will be marked black. When dry it may be ironed.

Print with a mixture of

1 part by volume	iron acetate liquor
8 parts by volume	thickening

Tragacanth for screen printing, British gum for block printing. Sodium alginate thickenings are not suitable.

The black colour is developed by simple exposure to the air. Hang the material up for a night and a day to allow the reaction time to complete itself, or accelerate the process by steaming for one hour.

Rinse thoroughly in cold running water, wash in hot soapy water, and finally rinse in cold running water.

This antique recipe gives a lovely velvety black, absolutely fast to light and to washing.

BASIC DYESTUFFS

for cotton and viscose rayon

Dissolve

10 grams	dyestuff, in a mixture of
50 grams	Glydote B (I.C.I.) or Kromofax (U.S.A.)
100 grams	acetic acid (40%)
170 ccs (6 ozs)	hot water

When dissolved, add

20 grams	tartaric acid, then stir the solution into
600 grams	thickening (tragacanth or gum arabic)

Leave to cool.

When cold, add very slowly, stirring all the time

50 grams	tannin/acetic (1 : 1) solution

This item is made by dissolving

25 grams	tannic acid powder, in
25 grams	acetic acid 25%

Leave the printed material to dry, then steam for one hour.

Then immerse for thirty seconds in a fixing bath deep enough to cover the material, consisting of

10 grams	tartar emetic (poison) per litre (34 ozs) of warm water, 50°C (120°F)

Rinse thoroughly in cold running water.

Fabrics printed with basic dyes must never be boiled.

BASIC DYESTUFFS

recipe for printing on silk

Dissolve

25 grams	dyestuff, in a mixture of

25 grams	glycerine
100 grams	acetic acid 40%
275 ccs (9·5 ozs)	hot water

Stir the solution into

| 500 grams | thickening (tragacanth or gum arabic) |

Finally add a solution of

| 25 grams | tartaric acid, dissolved in |
| 50 grams | water |

Leave the printed material to dry, then steam for one hour.
Rinse thoroughly in cold running water.
Fabrics printed with basic dyes must never be boiled.

ACID DYESTUFFS
for natural silk and wool

Paste together

| 40 grams | dyestuff |
| 50 grams | glycerine |

Add

| 300 ccs (10 ozs) | boiling water |

Boil the mixture if necessary until the colour is completely dissolved.
Stir the solution into

| 600 grams | thickening (tragacanth or gum arabic) |

Leave to cool.
When cold add

| 50 grams | tartaric acid solution (1:1) |

This last item is made by dissolving

| 25 grams | tartaric acid, in |
| 25 grams | water |

Leave the printed fabric to dry, then steam for one hour.
Rinse thoroughly in cold running water.
Wash carefully in warm water, 40°C (105°F), containing a little Stergene or Teepol (U.K.),
Synthrapol or Duponol (U.S.A.).
Rinse off in cold running water.

ACID DYESTUFFS
for silk and wool
Another recipe using Manutex (U.K.) or Keltex (U.S.A.) thickening

Paste together

| 20 grams | dyestuff |
| 50 grams | glycerine |

Add

| 200 ccs (7 ozs) | boiling water |

Boil until dissolved.
Leave to cool.

When cool, stir into

660 grams	Manutex or Keltex thickening

Finally add a solution of

20 grams	ammonium oxalate, dissolved in
50 ccs (2 ozs)	water

Steam and wash as in the previous recipe.

SOLUBLE-VAT DYESTUFFS
for cotton and linen
Recipe 1   The Nitrite Process

Mix together

50 grams	dyestuff
50 grams	urea
50 ccs (2 ozs)	water

Heat up to 80°C (175°F) if necessary to dissolve.

Stir solution into

800 grams	Manutex (U.K.) or Keltex (U.S.A.) thickening

Finally stir in

50 grams	sodium nitrite solution (30%)

Leave the printed fabric to dry, and then if possible steam for fifteen minutes. This steaming gives better penetration, but is not absolutely necessary.

Then immerse the fabric for three seconds in a developing bath containing

20 ccs	sulphuric acid (168° Tw), in
1 litre (34 ozs)	water at 70°C (160°F)

CAUTION: Add the acid little by little to the water. Do not add water to acid. Wear rubber gloves and apron.

Stand the bath by an open window or under an extractor fan. Dangerous nitrous fumes are given off when the printed fabric enters the developing bath.

After development, hold the wet fabric out to the air for thirty seconds and then give it a thorough rinse in cold running water.

Then immerse the fabric for fifteen minutes in a boiling solution of ordinary soap. This treatment brings out the maximum brightness and fastness of the vat dyes.

Finish with a rinse in cold running water.

SOLUBLE-VAT DYESTUFFS
Recipe 2   The Sulphocyanide Process

Mix together

50 grams	dyestuff
50 grams	Glydote B (I.C.I.) or Kromofax (U.S.A.)
50 grams	urea
150 ccs (5 ozs)	hot water

Heat up to 80°C (175°F) if necessary to dissolve.

Stir solution into

550 grams	thickening (tragacanth or Manutex (U.K.) or Keltex (U.S.A.)

When quite cold add

50 grams	ammonium sulphocyanide (50% solution)
80 grams	sodium chlorate (10% solution)
20 grams	ammonium vanadate (1% solution)

This recipe should be made up fresh before use.

Leave the printed fabric to dry, and then steam for half an hour.

Rinse thoroughly in cold running water.

Boil for fifteen minutes in a soap solution.

Rinse off again in cold running water.

REACTIVE DYESTUFFS

for cotton, linen and viscose rayon

Mercerized cotton gives the best colour value. The Procion recipe which follows is typical of this group.

Dissolve

100 grams	urea, in
425 ccs (14·5 ozs)	water

Warm up to, but not beyond, 70°C (160°F). Stir until dissolved.

This solution is used to dissolve

50 grams	dyestuff

When the dyestuff has dissolved, the solution is slowly and carefully stirred into 400 grams Manutex thickening prepared as follows:

Dissolve

4 grams	Calgon, in
56 ccs (2 ozs)	water at 60°C (140°F)

Add to this solution

320 ccs (11 ozs)	cold water

Stir this solution briskly with a fork, and pour in slowly as a fine drift

20 grams	Manutex R.S. or Keltex (U.S.A.)

Continue stirring for five minutes and then leave for at least fifteen minutes until the paste has thickened. Better still, make the Manutex paste the day before it is wanted. Then add to the thickened colour

10 grams	Resist Salt L (I.C.I.) or Sitol flakes (U.S.A.), and finally, just before printing
15 grams	sodium bicarbonate

Leave the printed fabric to dry, and then fix by one of the following methods.

1 Steaming for ten minutes or longer.

2 Baking for five minutes at 140°C (285°F) in an electric oven with temperature control.

3 Ironing the back for five minutes at 140°C with a thermostatically controlled iron, or with a steam iron.

4 Air hanging for forty-eight hours in a warm, humid atmosphere. For this process superior results are obtained if the 15 grams sodium bicarbonate is replaced by a mixture of 10 grams sodium bicarbonate and 5 grams sodium carbonate.

66

5 Air hanging (alternative method). For this method the fabric must first be prepared by soaking it for half a minute in a cold solution of 20 grams sodium carbonate per litre (34 ozs) of water. The fabric is then squeezed, dried and ironed. After printing, the fabric is hung up for forty-eight hours in a warm, humid atmosphere.

After fixing, rinse very thoroughly in cold running water until the water runs clear.

Finally, boil the fabric for five minutes in a solution of Lissapol ND (I.C.I.) or Synthrapol (U.S.A.), 2 grams per litre (34 ozs). If this solution becomes highly coloured, it must be thrown away and replaced by a fresh bath.

If the washing of Procion (reactive) prints is not done with great perseverance and thoroughness the whites are apt to be stained.

PIGMENT COLOURS

These are not true dyes, but fine solids suspended in a binder. The modern pigment colours based on an oil-in-water emulsion leave the fabric less stiff than some of the earlier types. They are easy to use, and can be applied to almost any fibre, provided that the fibre itself is not injured by the fixation process. These colours offer the amateur the easiest means of printing on man-made fibres. Two typical recipes follow:

Recipe 1   Polyprint Colours (U.K.) or Acco-Lite (U.S.A.)

If possible prepare the fabric by steeping it overnight in a solution of one teaspoonful of malt extract per gallon of warm water. Next morning wash the fabric, dry and iron it ready for printing.

Mix together cold

	DEEP SHADE	MEDIUM SHADE	PALE SHADE	
Polyprint colour	10	4	0·5	parts by volume
Polyprint binder	90	96	99·5	parts by volume
	100	100	100	

The flow of the paste can also be adjusted by additions of Manutex thickener.

Allow each colour to dry before overprinting with the next.

Leave the finished material to dry overnight before fixing.

Fix by baking for three minutes at 280°F in an electric oven. If there is no oven, fix by ironing the back of the fabric with an iron set at 'cotton' heat.

Polyprint and Acco-Lite colours can also be fixed by steaming for one hour.

Rinse and wash in the usual way or, if preferred, the material may be left unwashed.

Recipe 2   'Tinolite' Colours (U.K.)

Mix together cold

1 part by volume   'Tinolite' colour

19 parts by volume   'Tinolite' Printing Binder CM 18%

Too rapid drying can be prevented by the addition of 1%–3% glycerine to the printing paste.

The flow of the paste can also be adjusted by additions of Manutex thickener.

'Tinolite' Colours (U.S.A.)

Mix together cold under high-speed agitation to make 150 ozs

124 ozs	water
1 oz	ammonia 28%
4 ozs (liquid measure)	'Tinolite' Extender Concentrate 777A
12 ozs	'Tinolite' Binder 760
2·5–12 ozs	'Tinolite' colour

Add colour only after all other ingredients are thoroughly mixed.

Allow the printed material to dry thoroughly, and then fix by baking for three to four minutes at 300°F. With lower temperatures a longer curing time is necessary.

When printing 'Tinolite' colours alone, drying and curing are the only indispensable operations. There is no need to soap the material after printing.

This selection of recipes is no more than a working introduction to a vast and labyrinthine subject: the standard reference book on textile printing has 1,064 pages. Some of the dye families are so large that it is not possible to give one recipe to suit all the individual members. The recipes given here are believed to be the most useful because within their limitations they allow the printer the widest possible range of colour. The printer who wants to go deeper will quickly find that he must learn more recipes, it may be to cover a small group of colours, or even one single colour within the same dye family. Faced with this situation, some beginners lose heart. They should remember that some races have found all they need for centuries in one colour – indigo. Good work does not depend on, and certainly does not follow from, a profusion of recipes.

7 · Steaming

So many printing recipes call for steam fixation that unless he is able to make and handle a steamer, the amateur is denying himself most of the craft. Steam fixation means simply exposing the printed material to the action of steam for a period long enough to complete the reaction in the chemicals concerned – say one hour. The process goes forward step by step during this time, and the full time must be given. If for any reason it is not possible to steam for an hour in one continuous period, the time can be subdivided; two half-hour periods equal one hour, and so on. If the steaming time is exceeded this does no harm, unless the steamer boils dry. Some craftsmen like to give double the recommended time.

A steamer should be large enough to accommodate a reasonable length of material in such a way that it can be reached by the steam, and yet is protected against wet. Splashes will leap up from the boiling water, drips will fall from above, and the inside walls of the container will stream with condensation. If the material gets wet, the print will run. If the

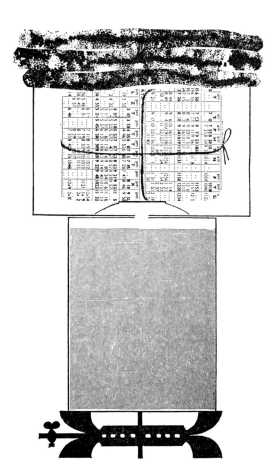

FIG 4 'Cake-tin' steamer

material is so well protected that the steam cannot get at it, fixation will be incomplete, and the print will run in the wash.

The water capacity should be large enough to allow for at least one hour's boiling without running dry. To be effective, a steamer should be capable of converting 2 pints (40 ozs) of water to steam per hour for every cubic foot capacity of the steam chamber.

The smallest steamer consists of two tins standing one on top of the other. The lower tin should be about 5 inches in diameter by about 7 inches deep, and a half-inch hole should be punched through the centre of the lid. The upper tin should be not less than 9 inches in diameter by 5 inches deep, and a half-inch hole should be punched through the centre of the bottom.

The lower tin is filled with water to within half an inch of the top, and stood on the gas ring or burner. When the water is boiling and not before, the upper tin is lowered into place so that the steam passes up through the two punched holes. The hole in the floor of the upper tin is now covered with an inverted saucer which acts as a steam spreader, and provides a dry resting place for the cloth parcel. The parcel must be very neatly made, and carefully set down on the inverted saucer in such a way that no part of the wrappings or string touches the sides or floor of the tin. Lastly, the open top of the top tin is covered with three or four circular pads of thick carpet underfelt trimmed to a diameter about 2 inches greater than the tin. These pads act as lagging or insulation and allow the steam to escape. It does not matter if the underside of the pads touch the cloth parcel. The metal tin lid is not used.

A steamer of this size can run for one hour without boiling dry. If the parcel is very carefully made, 4 yards of printed material can be accommodated.

Packing up the material to go in the steamer needs to be done with care. If the parcel is too tight, the steam will not get inside, if too loose the outside may touch the tin. If the material is folded up just as it is, the printed parts are likely to transfer an offset print or ghostly image to the part of the material against which they are folded. The best method is to spread the material out on the table and cover the printed surface with scrim (an open-weave jute) or clean newspaper; this will prevent any offset printing. Then, beginning at one end, roll up the material and scrim together. This will give a roll with a length equal to the width of the printed material and a diameter of about 3 inches. Flatten this roll by leaning on it with the palms of the hands, and then coil it up from one end like a fire hose or a Catherine wheel. Tie up the coil with raffia or string, and finish with a bow. This is to make it easy to open the parcel quickly as soon as it comes out of the steamer.

The disadvantage of this arrangement is that it takes some time for the steam to penetrate to the inside of the parcel and there is a danger that the fixation may be uneven. It is for this reason that some craftsmen steam their material for double the recommended time. The method begins by steaming for one hour in the ordinary way. At the end of the hour, the parcel is taken out and immediately opened. It is then rolled up again starting from the other end of the material, so that what was in the inside of the parcel for the first hour is on the outside for the second. Whilst this is being done, more water should be added to the steamer and brought to the boil.

A larger steamer can be made from an ordinary galvanized iron dustbin or garbage can. Four inches of water in the bottom will produce plenty of steam. The dustbin or garbage can may be propped up on bricks over a large gas ring or burner or over an outdoor fire. Alternatively, electric immersion heaters can be used: one dustbin or garbage can will need two $1\frac{1}{2}$-kilowatt kettle heaters. The outside of the steamer should be lagged, if possible, with a jacket of asbestos or glass wool (fibreglass insulating material).

A few inches above the level of the water there should be a perforated tray or sieve on which rest several layers of sacking or old felt cut to the same diameter as the dustbin or garbage can. This is a baffle to intercept any splashes thrown up by the boiling water.

The printed material is wrapped up in the usual way, and suspended in the space above the baffle. If there is only one parcel, the easiest method is to hang it simply from a stick resting across the mouth of the dustbin or garbage can. Larger loads can be carried on galvanized-wire or stainless-steel baskets or sieves supported by hooks. Several of these baskets can be arranged one above the other. The baskets should be well lined with pads of felt or sacking, and if there are to be several baskets arranged in tiers, the printed material should be protected by pads above as well as below. No part of the basket or of the pads should touch the sides of the steamer.

The ordinary dustbin or garbage can lid is the source of a continuous downpour of condensed water, and cannot be used without modification. The easiest remedy is to fill the conical space underneath with a great thickness of soft lagging material, holding it in place with a tightly tied cover of sacking. Or the lid can be dispensed with altogether, and replaced by several thick pads of felt supported on a simple frame. The steamer must not be hermetically sealed. Whatever covering is used, it must allow for the free escape of the steam and the volatile by-products given off during the process of fixation.

The technique of steaming may be summarized as follows:

1   Leave the printed material until the colour is dry. If it is not convenient to do the steaming at once, it can be left. So long as the material is kept dry, it will come to no harm. Where several colours have been overprinted on the same piece of material, one steaming at the end will fix them all: it is not necessary to fix each colour separately.

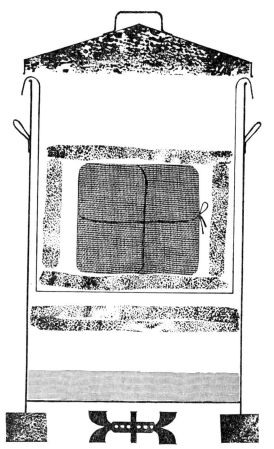

FIG 5   Dustbin or garbage can steamer

2   Wrap up the material in scrim or newspaper. Scrim is better than newspaper because its open weave allows the steam to penetrate more freely. The same piece can be used over and over again. Newspaper is less bulky, and is perfectly satisfactory for small parcels in the little cake-tin steamer. The newspaper ink will not mark the fabric. Always make the parcel as loose as the space allows.

3   Bring the water to the boil in the steamer, and never put in the parcel until the steam is coming up vigorously. With the dustbin or garbage can steamer, the action of lifting the lid and putting in the parcel must be very quickly done, or a lot of steam will be lost. It is worth rehearsing this movement until the time is cut down to less than two seconds.

4   Steam for the recommended time or, if preferred, for longer. Two separate half-hour periods are the equivalent of one period of an hour.

5   Remove the parcel from the steamer and open it out immediately. It is essential that this should be done every time a parcel comes out of the steamer. The reason is that at this moment the material will be full of steam, and if this is left to cool it will condense to water and may cause the print to run. When the parcel is opened straight from the steamer, steam will be seen to rise from the printed surface and the material will be hot but dry.

6   The fixation should now be complete, and the material ready for its first long rinse and wash. The printed areas still carry all the gum thickening and dye chemicals in excess of the proportion that has actually entered the fibre. To remove all this is a lengthy process requiring care and attention. It may take an hour or even longer. Once the material has been put in the water, the process must be carried right through to the end: if it is stopped half-way, the excess colour will most probably stain the whites. The printer's responsibilities do not end until he has completed this first wash. If it is not convenient to wash the newly steamed material at once, it can be put aside in a dry place until time can be spared.

8 · Block making

Any office rubber stamp would make an excellent block for textile printing: in every detail it is just what a block should be. The printing surface is perfectly flat, and the unwanted parts are deeply hollowed out. The material is reasonably robust, is not attacked by the printing colour, and is easy to clean. Behind the rubber is a strong, rigid backing to distribute the pressure, and a comfortable hand-hold.

Blocks for fabric printing can be made in either of two ways. In the first, the printing surface is cut into with a knife or gouge to remove the unwanted, or white parts of the pattern. In the second, a printing surface is built up by adding projections to the backing material. It is the difference between carving and modelling.

The simplest carved block is made from a large potato or any similar root. Cut the potato

PLATE 25 Lino block and stencil by Phyllis Barron
'Indigosol' dyes on French velveteen

PLATE 26 Hanging or coverlet (Palampore)
Coromandel Coast, *c* 1640
Freehand painting and drawing
Wax resist, indigo, madder and other vegetable dyes on cotton

74   *Victoria and Albert Museum: Crown copyright reserved*

PLATE 27 Freehand painting
Roro Bay territory, Papua, 1962
Pigments and vegetable stains on bark cloth (tapa)

PLATE 28 Freehand painting by June Barker
Flour paste resist
'Indigosol' dyes on cotton

PLATE 29 Block printing at its best
Border of Indian shawl
Early 19th century (?)
Mineral and vegetable colours on madder-dyed cotton

76

PLATE 30 Block made by Fred Gardiner
Copper and *lignum vitae* pegs in pear wood

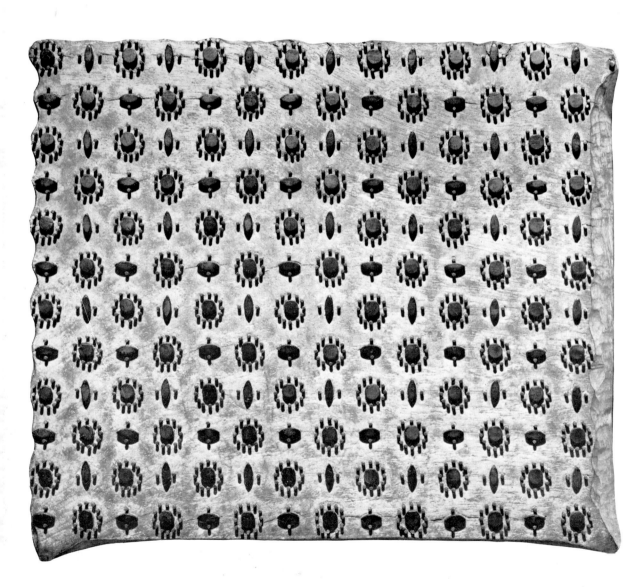

PLATE 31 Print from the opposite block
Iron liquor on galled cotton

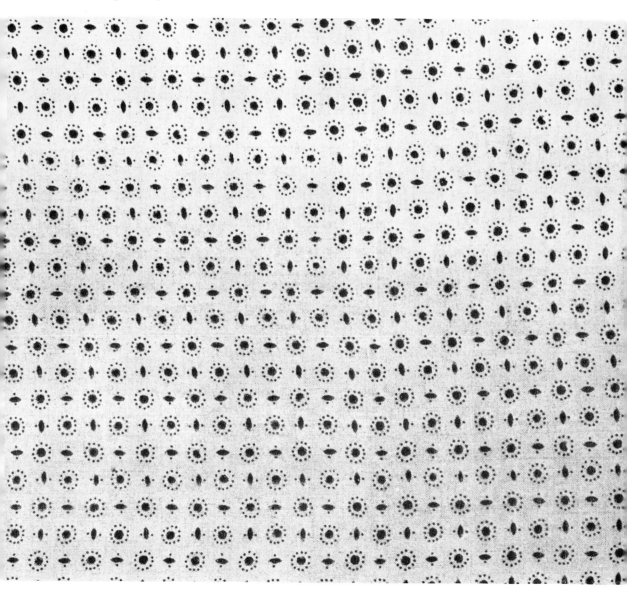

PLATE 32 Amateur screen printer at work

FIG 6   Linocut by 12-year-old girl

in half. Use a long knife, and cut as straight as possible, because the cut surface will be the printing surface and this must be flat. Any unevenness in the cut can be remedied by grinding the surface against a flat gritty stone. The white parts of the pattern can be cut away with a small sharp knife or gouge. The cuts should have a V section and be as deep and clean as possible. The potato makes an excellent introduction to the craft because it shows so clearly how a tiny, apparently insignificant unit, can acquire a grandeur by the simple act of repetition.

Linoleum is a useful substance. It has a flat surface, it is cheap, strong and washable, it has no grain and can be cut in any direction. For printing on fabric, a lino-cut must be mounted on a stiff backing block about one inch thick. This can be done either before or after the pattern is cut. The best backing is a sandwich of waterproof plywood. Ordinary deal plank (pine board) will warp and split along the grain. Apply a generous coat of waterproof glue to the hessian (fabric) at the back of the lino, and to the surface of the plywood block. Bring the glued surfaces together, and hold under a bookbinder's, or nipping press until the glue is set.

Unfortunately for the fabric printer, linoleum has one disadvantage: it contains a large amount of oil. All the dye-printing colours are watery fluids, and the oily surface of the lino rejects them. The result is seen in the print as a characteristic mottled film. Experienced designers know how to exploit this, but to most beginners the mottling is a source of bitter resentment.

The oily surface can be subdued in a number of ways, of which the quickest is to hold the block face down against a sheet of medium (No 2) sandpaper, and grind with circular strokes using considerable pressure, as if cleaning the doorstep. This will produce a dense texture of fine scratches. The sandpaper must rest against a hard, flat surface: if it is held in the hand, the surface of the block will become rounded.

Another method is to apply a coat of flocking to the printing surface. This is done after the pattern has been cut. Flocking powder is a fine chaff or fluff derived from wool or rayon, and it is held to the surface of the lino by an adhesive known as flocking mordant. The result is supposed to resemble the nap or pile of velvet.

A small rubber inking roller will be needed, an inking slab, and a fine sieve which may be improvised from perforated zinc sheeting. Using the little roller, apply an even film of flocking mordant to the surface of the lino. Flocking mordant consists of an oil paint made with an excess of varnish. Straight copal varnish can be used instead, provided it is left to thicken in an open saucer for a day or so before being used. The word 'mordant' is misleading: it has nothing to do with the mordant dyes, and it is not corrosive. The word comes, together with the process, from the painting and decorating trade.

While the mordant is still wet, shake down on to it a thick deposit of flocking powder. Use the sieve for this, not that there are any impurities in the flocking powder, but in order to break up the lumps into which it tends to gather itself. Now lower a flat board on to the deposit of flocking powder, and apply gentle hand pressure. This helps to embed the powder in the mordant. Leave the coated block in a dry place until the mordant has set. The surplus powder can then be brushed off and returned to the container for another time.

The coat of flocking must be renewed as often as it wears off, and whenever the block is to be used with another colour.

Flocking is no more than a poor imitation of the felt-covered blocks of the old printers. To make one of these, a piece of fine felt or woollen cloth is glued with waterproof glue to the surface of the block, and the white parts cut out with a sharp knife, cutting through the felt and deep into the block. A gouge cannot be used when cutting felt. This type of block is by far the best answer to the mottling problem, but is not suited to fine line work. For fine work, the old printers used blocks of seasoned cherry or pear wood. They were carved with knife and gouge, and lasted a hundred years. Enthusiasts can still buy seasoned cherry and pear wood. Beginners might like to test their skill on whitewood (sycamore): this is easy to cut, and makes an excellent block.

Turning now to the construction of built-up blocks, the first requirement is a base with a flat surface on which to build. For small blocks, short lengths of 2×1-inch deal (pine board) might be used, but for anything larger it is worth making a lamination or sandwich of waterproof plywood one inch thick.

Simple little blocks can be made by glueing felt patterns to the surface of the backing. Hat felt is exactly right for this purpose. It can be cut to shape with scissors, and is thick enough to stand out well from the backing. In this style of work there is no gouging out of the white parts of the pattern: everything depends on the applied material being thick enough to give a printing surface well clear of the backing.

Other material can be used in place of hat felt; for example, leather, rubber, foam sheeting, pipe cleaners, glass fibre, plywood, hardboard, matchsticks, string, pearl barley. A waterproof glue such as Evo-Stik 'Impact' (U.K.) or Sobo (U.S.A.) must be used. The print quality resulting from these items is as varied as may be imagined.

For a change cylindrical blocks might be made, like the cylinder seals of Babylon. If we thread a long nail as an axle through the centre hole of a cotton reel (spool), we have made a primitive type of roller. Larger rollers can be made from rolling pins. The surface can be decorated by carving or applied pattern. Inking and printing are done by rolling.

All blocks designed for fabric printing must be considerably more bold and open than blocks designed for paper. The fine, shallow lines of the wood engraver would be filled up by the watery printing paste. For safety, no part of the pattern should be narrower than a sixteenth of an inch. All cuts should have a V section, and all unwanted parts should be cut away deeply or they will pick up the colour. The outside edges always give trouble in this way, and they should be trimmed back hard.

Work at a solid table and in a good light. The block can be supported by a carpenter's bench hook. This protects the table, and is better than any cramps (clamps). The basis is a

FIG 7   Bench hook

sheet of half-inch ply about 12 inches square. Across the upper surface at the far end is screwed and glued a piece of 2×1-inch deal the width of the ply. Across the under surface at the near edge is screwed and glued an identical piece of deal. The bench hook rests on the table with its underside piece of deal pressing against the table edge. The block lies on the bench hook and can be steadied as required by pressing it against the deal at the far end.

Never attempt to cut in the lap. Learn how to grip the block without getting the hand in the way of the cutting stroke. Cut fingers and spoilt blocks are caused by trying to work with blunt tools. A fine oil-stone should be kept on the bench, and the tools sharpened not once a year, but several times in an hour. Finish the back and sides of the blocks with sandpaper, and give two coats of shellac or varnish – this will make them easier to clean. During printing, large blocks are easier to hold if a small brass drawer handle is screwed to the back. This can be removed at the end of the printing and transferred to another block.

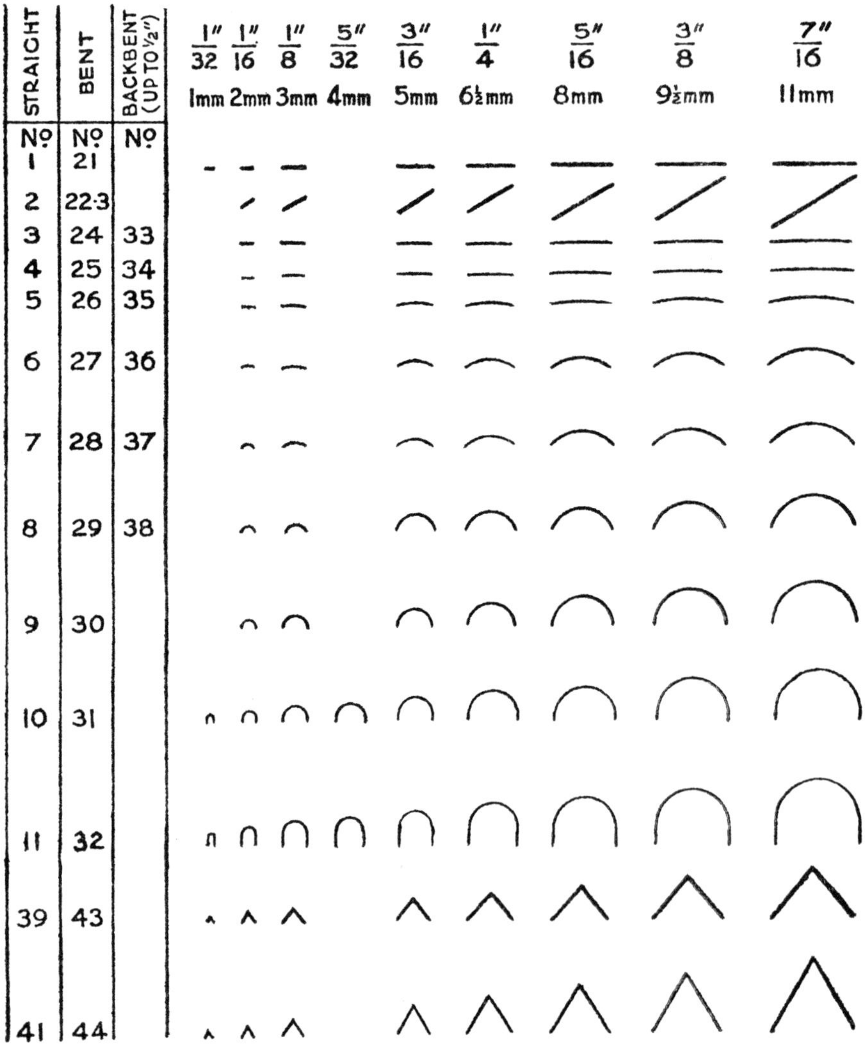

STRAIGHT	BENT	BACKBENT (UP TO ½")	$\frac{1''}{32}$ 1mm	$\frac{1''}{16}$ 2mm	$\frac{1''}{8}$ 3mm	$\frac{5''}{32}$ 4mm	$\frac{3''}{16}$ 5mm	$\frac{1''}{4}$ 6½mm	$\frac{5''}{16}$ 8mm	$\frac{3''}{8}$ 9½mm	$\frac{7''}{16}$ 11mm
No. 1	No. 21	No.									
2	22·3										
3	24	33									
4	25	34									
5	26	35									
6	27	36									
7	28	37									
8	29	38									
9	30										
10	31										
11	32										
39	43										
41	44										

FIG 8 Wood-carving tools

9 · Screen making

The silk screen process is a refinement of stencilling. The apparatus consists of a rectangular wooden frame across which silk or cotton organdie is tightly stretched. The silk has a special open weave through which printing colour can pass freely, as through a sieve. When lowered into contact with the surface to be printed, colour can be forced through the silk so as to print a flat rectangular shape corresponding to the size of the screen being used. If parts of the silk mesh have been clogged with a waterproof filler the colour will not be able to pass, and these places will show white in the print. The silk acts as an open surface on which the designer applies the negative or white parts of the pattern.

First attempts can be made with an old picture frame, but for more serious work special frames should be made. These can be used over and over again, and should last for years. Each colour will need a frame to itself, and there is everything to be said for making all the frames to a standard size. A frame 12 × 18 inches will take patterns of any shape or size up to about 10 × 12 inches.

The frame is made of straight-grained, knot-free softwood planed to $1\frac{1}{2} \times \frac{3}{4}$ inches. The two side walls should be 18 inches long, the two ends 12 inches. The saw cuts must be accurate: if they are not, the frame will not be square. Complicated corner joints are not necessary: butt-nailing with $1\frac{1}{2}$-inch panel pins and waterproof glue is quite strong enough. It is essential that the finished frame should lie flat against a flat surface. Any sign of warping or rocking must be corrected by planing. All the outside edges and corners should be well rounded with sandpaper, all the inner edges left sharp.

FIG 9   Screen print by Ian Harper taken from the monumental brass of Sir Robert de Septvans (d. 1306), St Mary's, Chartham, Kent

Larger frames can be made for special purposes, but it is hardly worth making anything smaller than the frame described. Trade printers use a frame to go across the whole width of the fabric in one. To print across fabric 36 inches wide, the screen would have to be not less than 44 inches long inside the frame. The screen used to print the brass rubbing was 7 feet long. Large frames should be made of 3×1-inch deal lying flat, that is, not up on edge as in the little frame. The corner joints should be half-cut, glued with waterproof glue, and screwed.

The best material to stretch across the frame is bolting silk, a natural silk with a very accurate and finely made open weave. It comes in several grades, of which 8 XX is the most useful. Unfortunately, bolting silk is expensive, and most beginners have to make do with cotton. A good quality organdie will not give trouble.

Fasten the silk to the frame with office staples, tacks, drawing pins, or waterproof glue. Casco Grade A casein glue or Sobo is just right for this purpose, as it is also for making the frames. If staples or tacks are used, the silk may become distorted as it tightens between them: with glue this cannot happen. The silk should be stretched as tight as possible by hand. Begin at two points opposite each other at the middle of the two long sides, then move to two points at the middle of the short ends. Work steadily out towards the corners, pulling always with the weave of the silk, never diagonally into the corners. Finish with a neat mitre lap (called a 'hospital corner' in the U.S.A.).

The tool used to press the colour through the silk is called a squeegee: it acts rather like a windscreen (windshield) wiper. Satisfactory prints can be made with a squeegee improvised from rubber draught-excluder (called 'stripping' in the U.S.A.) glued with an 'Impact' (U.K.) or Casco (U.S.A.) adhesive to the lower edge of a scrap of hardboard.

FIG 10 Improvised squeegee

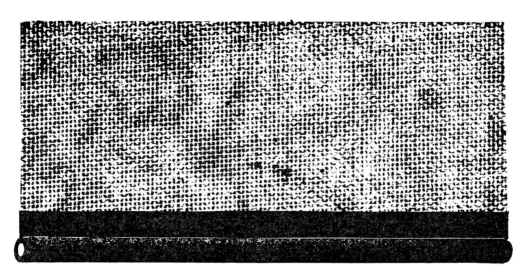

A professional squeegee is not difficult to make. The blade consists of black rubber strip $2 \times \frac{1}{4}$ inch, which is made for this purpose and sold by the foot run. The length of the blade must be just short of the interior width of the screen frame. In the 12×18-inch screen, the squeegee blade should be $11\frac{3}{4}$ inches long. The blade must be fixed in a straight wooden handle deep enough and so shaped as to give the printer a comfortable hand-hold. Projections at both ends of the handle should extend for about an inch beyond the length of the blade. These projections rest on the side walls of the screen frame when the squeegee is let go at the end of the stroke.

FIG 11　Squeegee

The easiest method of constructing a squeegee is to make a sandwich, with the rubber blade as the filling between two side pieces of softwood planed to $\frac{7}{8} \times \frac{3}{8}$ inch. Timber merchants in Great Britain sell this as 'door stop'. Running along the top edge of the sandwich there should be a third piece of door stop projecting 1 inch at both ends. The whole assembly can be made with 'Impact' (U.K.) or Sobo (U.S.A.) adhesive, and with no tools other than a tenon saw. All the edges of the wood should be well rounded with sandpaper, the rubber blade left sharp. If all the screen frames are made to the same size, only one squeegee will be needed to print them all.

The stroke of the squeegee covers the whole area of the screen from end to end, out and back, beginning and ending at one of the short ends. As it travels along, it sweeps before it a charge of printing colour, perhaps half a pint or more. In the middle of the stroke, the squeegee passes over the open parts of the pattern, and here it drives the colour through the silk and makes the print. At both ends of the stroke there must be a broad area of waterproofed silk on to which the colour can be swept, and where it will lie without coming through. In the jargon of the trade, these neutral areas are called 'harbours', 'wells' or 'banks'. Each harbour must be about 3 inches broad in small screens and proportionately more in large screens. In the 12×18-inch screen, the two harbours would together take up 6 inches of the silk (3 inches at each end). A small border, say 1 inch wide, running along the side walls must also be allowed for. With these deductions, this means that in the 12×18-inch screen the designer is left with an area of 10×12 inches for his pattern.

All designs for screen printing on fabric must be fully worked out on a master drawing, and this drawing must show not only one unit of the design, but the arrangement of the repeats all around it. The best way to do this is to set out a grid of guide lines accurately drawn at right-angles to each other. This grid will be used later on when marking out the fabric.

FIG 12   Screen printing grid

Before he can transfer his design to the silk, the printer must pause to decide which way round he intends to hold the screen during printing. The fabric will be fastened down on the long table, the printer will stand at the side of the table facing across it, and he will lower his screen on to the fabric immediately in front of him. Some printers set the screen down with the long side in line with the length of the fabric, others with the long side at right-angles to the length of the fabric; it depends on which style of squeegee stroke is preferred.

When this has been settled, the design can be transferred to the silk. Lower the screen on to the master drawing so that one unit of the repeat lies within the permitted working area. The drawing can be seen quite plainly through the silk, as through tracing paper. With a ball-point pen, trace the outlines of the master drawing on to the silk. On the outside of the frame make very accurate vertical ticks to show where the lines of the grid pass through. These ticks will later guide the screen to its place on the grid drawn on the fabric.

By far the simplest and most generally useful way to fill in the negative parts of the design is to paint them in free-hand with shellac. Half fill a screw-topped bottle with orange shellac flakes, cover with methylated spirit (grain or methyl alcohol), and shake. In about three days at room temperature, with occasional shaking, the flakes will have dissolved. The stiffness of the solution can be adjusted by adding more flakes or more solvent. Aim

88

for the consistency of hot syrup, not cold. Oil and colour merchants sell shellac ready for use in small bottles labelled 'Best Patent Knotting' (U.K.) or white shellac (U.S.A.).

Paint in all those parts where the colour is not to be allowed through, the parts that are to be white in the print. Whilst painting, prop the screen up on a vacant frame so that the silk is lifted clear of the table, or turn the screen right over and apply the shellac to the underside – it comes to the same thing. Give two or more coats so that the weave of the silk is really clogged, and no pinholes or 'holidays' can be seen when it is held up to the light.

The marginal area of silk surrounding the picture space must now be filled in, that is, the harbours at both ends and the narrow border running down the two long sides. It would be sufficient to fill this area with shellac, treating it as a negative part of the design, but there is another way.

Turn the screen right over, and cut four strips of newspaper as masks to cover the marginal area, two for the harbours, two for the side borders. Apply a liberal coat of casein glue to the newspaper strips and leave for ten minutes. During this time the newspaper will stretch. Now apply a second, thin, coat of glue, and lower the strips carefully into place on the underside of the silk, the word underside being understood to mean underside as the screen is held during printing. Smooth out the paper to remove any creases, and then

FIG 13   Newspaper masks on underside of screen

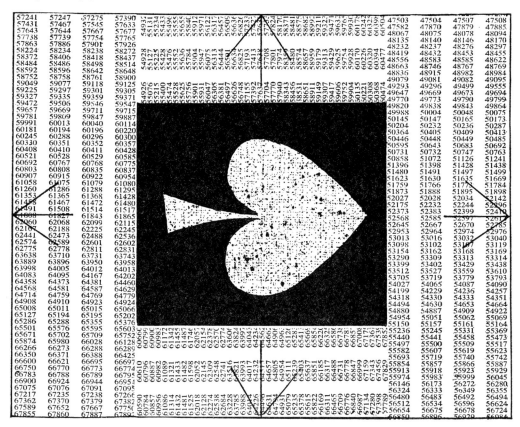

turn the screen over again to bring it right side up. With the tips of the fingers, go over all the marginal area, working with small circular strokes, and using some pressure. This will bring the glue up into the silk, and make a close union between silk and newspaper. Set the screen aside for the glue to dry. As it dries, the newspaper will contract, and stretch the silk as tight as a drum. Finish with two coats of shellac over all the marginal area, inside and out.

The technique of glueing paper masks to the underside of the silk can be used instead of shellac to make the pattern in the middle of the screen. Waterproof glue must be used. The paper may be anything from torn newspaper for large bold designs, to typing paper for fine-cut work.

A refinement of the cut-paper method has been introduced by Selectasine Silk Screens Ltd. Their Profilm (U.K.) or Nu-Film (U.S.A.) consists of two transparent sheets laminated together, the upper coated with shellac, and the backing sheet impregnated with wax. The Profilm is pinned over the master drawing, shellac side up, and the positive parts of the design cut out with a very sharp knife. The knife should cut through the upper sheet only, the positive parts being removed as they are cut, and leaving the backing sheet intact. When the cutting is done, a newly covered screen is lowered into place over the Profilm or Nu-Film sheet, and the inside of the silk pressed with an iron set at 'silk' heat. The heat of the iron softens the shellac film, and this becomes the adhesive holding the Profilm or Nu-Film to the silk. The waxed backing sheet is then carefully peeled off. After this, the marginal areas must be filled in as already described.

In the above methods the designer is working with the negative parts of the pattern. The so-called resist methods allow him to do the exact opposite. In these the positive parts are painted into the silk with some compound which acts as a temporary protective coating and is later removed. Water glass (sodium silicate) can be used for this, dissolved in its own weight of warm water.

Another recipe is:

1 part by volume	glycerine
2 parts by volume	gum arabic
3 parts by volume	french chalk

Paste to a fine cream and apply as a generous coat to the underside of the silk.

Leave to dry, and then brush all over the underside of the silk one or two coats of quick-drying lacquer.

When this is dry, turn the screen the right way up for printing. The pattern can now be seen on the inside as a whitish zone where the paste lies as a protective film between silk and lacquer.

Carry the screen across to the sink and fill it with warm water. After a time the paste will soften, and by gently scrubbing with a nail brush, the lacquer covering the positive parts will come away. The resist styles are suitable for bold brush work, but not for fine detail.

Whichever method is used to make the pattern, all screens should be finished by varnishing. Have ready a clean 2-inch brush, clear varnish, turpentine substitute, and three or four pieces of clean rag made up into bun shapes and damped, but not soaked, in turpentine substitute.

Turn the screen over and apply a full coat of varnish all over the underside of the silk. Turn the screen back again, as for printing, and prop it on a vacant frame so that the silk is held clear of the table. Now, taking one of the pieces of rag in the palm of the hand, wipe the inside of the silk with flat, sweeping strokes following the weave of the silk, up and down and across. The effect of this stroke is to draw the varnish out of the open parts of the pattern. Change to a fresh piece of rag and continue in the same way until the open parts really are clear. Hold the screen up to the light to make sure. Leave the finished screen lying horizontally in a warm airy place until the varnish is dry.

If preferred, the screen may be varnished on the inside. This is in some ways better, but in the case of cut paper stencils not easy to do: the rag used to clear the varnish from the underside is likely to lift and tear the stencil.

Varnishing adds an extra layer of protection to the negative parts of the screen and helps to fill the pinholes. It also impregnates the silk threads with a dilute varnish, leaving them waterproof and glassy. During printing the colour flows more smoothly and is less likely to clog. Washing the screen after use takes half the time.

10 · Printing

If the design calls for a dyed background colour, the dyeing must be done before the printing. It is not reasonable to expect any printing to withstand one hour's boiling in a dyebath.

First attempts at block printing can be made on a kitchen table padded with many thicknesses of newspaper, but for serious work it is better to make a special printing table. A useful working top can be made from chipboard, blockboard or plywood sold by builders' merchants or lumber yards in standard sheets 8×4 feet, and in thicknesses from $\frac{1}{2}$ to 1 inch. All printing tables should be as long and as heavy as the room allows. A permanent table can be made from two or more 8-foot boards end to end, using the 1-inch thickness. Where space is limited, a portable top can be made from one board, using the $\frac{1}{2}$-inch thickness.

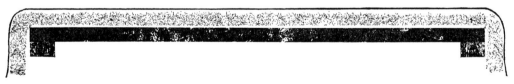

FIG 14   Portable table top

Screw and glue a strengthening frame of 2×1-inch deal to the underside of the chipboard or plywood, running round all four sides. Pad the top with one thickness of carpet underfelt, and cover this with waterproof sheeting (plastic or rubber) stretched tight and tacked all round. American cloth (so-called in Great Britain) will do, but for heavy wear it is cheaper in the long run to buy the vulcanized rubber ply sheeting manufactured for the trade. The 52-inch width is just right for tacking to a table 48 inches wide.

The fabric to be printed must be stretched out flat on the table, and fixed so that it cannot move. Pins must not be used. The following method is satisfactory, and can be managed single handed.

Materials required:

Two rough deal battens (wood strips) 2×1 inch in section, and each as long as the printing table is wide.

Four 3-inch G cramps (clamps)

Ten drawing pins (or tacks)

$\frac{5}{8}$-inch wide Sellotape (U.K.) or masking tape (U.S.A.)

Spread the fabric out on the printing table, and lay the battens across, one at each end. Fasten one end of the fabric to its batten with five of the drawing pins, and cramp the ends of this batten firmly and squarely to the sides of the printing table.

Pin the free end of the fabric to the second batten, and pull to stretch the fabric. Keep the fabric stretched, and cramp the ends of the second batten to the side of the printing table. Stick down the two selvages with Sellotape or masking tape, release the cramps and remove the battens. Stick down the two ends of the fabric with Sellotape or masking tape.

The screen printer now has to mark out on the fabric in faint pencil lines the rectangular grid on which his repeats are to be arranged. This grid is copied directly from the grid on the master drawing.

Cramp a long straight batten to the table top, running parallel with the selvage. Mark along the selvage faint pencil ticks at the spacing of the grid lines running across the fabric. Draw these lines across the fabric, using a large set square (or T-square) held up against the long straight batten. Release the cramps and remove the batten.

Now go to the two ends of the fabric and mark the position of the centre line, and the spacing of the longitudinal grid lines running parallel with it. Draw in these lines, using the long batten as a straightedge. All this marking out must be done with the utmost care and accuracy; in screen printing the fitting of the repeats depends upon it.

The block printer can usually dispense with a drawn-out grid. All he needs is a starting line across one end of the fabric at right-angles to the selvage. He sets his first row of prints to this line, and from then on works his way slowly down the fabric, fitting by eye each succeeding row to the row just printed.

As with the office rubber stamp, the fabric printer's blocks are inked by pressing them against a pad saturated with the colour. Dye printing colour cannot be applied to the block by roller. The simplest inking pad consists of thin foam sheeting lying on a flat sheet of glass or slate. Or a pad can be made from a sheet of chipboard or plywood about 12 inches square. Pad the top with one thickness of carpet underfelt, and cover this with waterproof sheeting stretched tight and tacked all round. This assembly is washable, and can be used over and over again. To fit it for printing, a piece of woollen material, such as blazer cloth, is pinned over the waterproof cover. This holds the colour during printing, and at the end it is taken off and washed ready for another time. The professional block printer uses

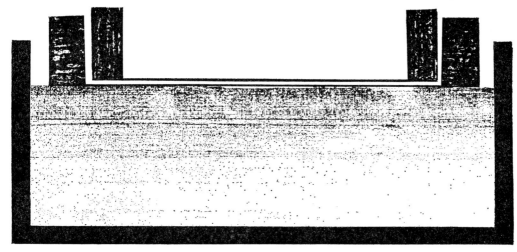

FIG 15   Block-printer's 'sieve'

an arrangement much more elaborate, but much more satisfactory than either of the above.

The outer container, which may be a deep enamel or polythene (U.K.) or polyethylene (U.S.A.) tray, is nearly filled with flour or Manutex or Keltex paste made to the consistency of thin jelly. Floating on this is a shallow tray made by stretching a sheet of waterproof material, such as polythene, polyethylene or rubber, tightly across a rectangular wooden frame. Resting inside this tray is an inner container called a sieve. The sieve consists of a piece of woollen cloth stretched tightly across a light wooden frame. Printing colour is poured into the sieve, and brushed out to an even film with a large distemper or paint brush. The sieve is the saturated surface. Cushioned on the jelly bath it is both flat and resilient.

Set out on a trolley or wheeled table the inking pad, brush and colour. It is asking for trouble to have them on the printing table. Saturate the inking pad with colour: it will need at least half a pint to start it off. Brush it out flat and even. Press the face of the block gently against the pad, lift it, rotate it through a quarter turn (from north to west), and press it down again. This is to equalize any possible unevenness of colour in the pad. After every print the block must be inked again in this way.

Make a few test prints on newspaper. Small blocks can be printed by hand pressure alone. Large blocks are printed with the help of a mallet. The left hand holds the block steady, and the right hand grasps the mallet. The blow is delivered vertically downwards by the butt end of the shaft. One blow near each corner of the block should be sufficient, and to maintain an even weight right down the fabric the same blows must be given to each print.

Where the design requires two or more colours to be overprinted, it is best to print the whole of the material with the first colour before beginning the second. This gives the first time to dry, and avoids the trouble of two wet colours running into each other, or of the first colour coming up into the block and dirtying the second colour.

Wash the blocks thoroughly at the end of every printing session: never leave them with colour on them. After washing, mop them dry with an old towel and stand them up in a warm, airy place – not on a radiator or near a fire.

Leave the printed material to dry where it is, or hang it up on a suspended drying rack. This should not be attempted if there is any danger of smearing the print. When dry, steam.

It is possible for block printers to print long pieces of fabric even though they have only a small table.

Materials required:

The fabric to be printed.

A piece of unbleached cotton (the 'backgrey'), as long and as wide as the fabric to be printed.

Two broom handles.

Two rough deal battens or wood strips as long as the table is wide.

Four 3-inch G cramps (clamps).

Suspended drying rack.

Roll the fabric on to one of the broom handles. Roll the backgrey on to the other. Spread out the backgrey with the free end at the left-hand end of the table, and the roll at the right-hand end. Spread out the fabric on top of the backgrey in the same way. Smooth out any creases with the palms of the hands, and fasten the material down by cramping the two battens across the table, one over the free ends, the other as near as possible to the two rolls. Print the area between the two battens.

FIG 16   Block printing on a small table

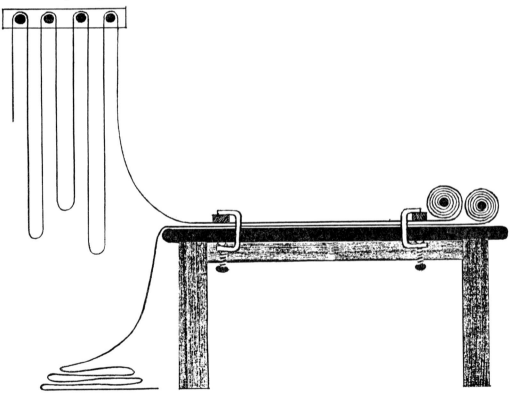

94

Loosen the cramps, grasp the free ends of fabric and backgrey and pull so as to unwind the next area to be printed. Allow the free end of the backgrey to fall on the floor. Hoist the free end of the printed fabric on to the suspended drying rack. Cramp down the battens for the next area.

In this way, bit by bit, the fabric is unwound from its broom handle, rather like the ribbon on a typewriter. The function of the backgrey is to absorb any colour that comes through to the back of the fabric; without it the table top would quickly become dirty. At the end of the job the backgrey can be washed ready for another time.

This procedure cannot be followed in screen printing. In screen printing the table must be as long as the fabric to be printed, the fabric must be fastened down and a firm and accurate grid drawn, and nothing must be moved until all the colours are printed.

All this is necessary because the area of the screen is larger than the area of the print made by it. When one unit of the repeat has been printed, the printer cannot immediately print the unit next to it. If he did, the wet colour from the first unit would print itself up on to the underside of the screen, and in due course this would be transferred to the fabric further along as an offset image. This means that the printer has to work up the fabric printing alternate units, 1, 3, 5, 7, 9. When he has reached the end, the first prints may have dried sufficiently to allow him to fill in the empty spaces, 2, 4, 6, 8, 10.

The actual printing is made very much quicker and easier if the printer can have a friend on the other side of the table to help him. With two people sighting from opposite sides, the screen can be lowered more accurately into position on the grid lines.

Before starting work on the fabric, take a number of trial prints on newspaper. This will help to 'wet out' the silk, and will also show where any pinholes need last-minute repair. It will also show if any adjustments are needed in the consistency of the printing colour.

The two styles of squeegee stroke are as follows:

1   Stand facing across the table, and lower the screen with its long axis at right-angles to the length of the fabric. Drop the squeegee into the screen an inch or two out from the near end. Pour colour into the space between the squeegee and the near end of the screen. Grip the squeegee in both hands and sweep the colour to the far end. Lift the squeegee, slide the blade behind the ridge of colour, and pull it back home to its starting point. During the stroke the helper can steady the frame by pressing down on the two corners nearest to him.

2   Stand as before, and lower the screen with its long axis in line with the length of the fabric. If right handed, drop the squeegee into the screen an inch or two out from the left-hand end. Pour colour into the space between the squeegee and the left-hand end of the screen. Hold the screen steady by pressing down on the near left-hand corner. Grip the squeegee in the right hand and sweep the colour – a backhand stroke – to the right-hand end. Lift the squeegee, slide the blade behind the ridge of colour, and sweep it back home to its starting point. This stroke can be managed single handed.

Handling a squeegee is a skilled art, acquired only by experience. The movement must be relaxed, unhurried, smooth and without hesitation. The blade has to press the colour through the open parts of the pattern, and leave the inside of the silk clean. It is rather like spreading butter on bread, and trying to scrape off as much as possible with the same stroke.

Each colour must be left to dry before the next is printed. When the last colour is dry, the fabric can be lifted from the table and hung up in a dry place until there is time to steam it.

All screens must be washed very thoroughly after every printing session, scrubbed gently and hosed vigorously until perfectly clear. If printing colour is allowed to dry hard in the silk, it may not be possible to remove it. After washing, mop the screen with an old towel, and stand to dry in a warm airy place, not too near a fire or household heater.

11 · Tie-dyeing

Tie-dyeing is not a printing process and cannot be done by machine. Consequently, tie-dyed material never appears in the shops. It is one of the most primitive methods of pattern dyeing, and has a unique quality depending on the free running of the dye in the fibre. The work can be done by bed-ridden invalids and by little children; it requires no apparatus, not even a table.

The craftsman takes his fabric and gathers it up in places, binding these tightly with raffia. When the tied-up fabric is put in the dyebath the dye is unable to penetrate the bindings. At the end of the dyeing period the fabric is taken out and washed, and the bindings removed. The protected areas then emerge as a pattern of white against a dyed background.

Raffia is the best material for binding, but on simple designs small rubber bands save time. It is better to buy both these items by weight, not in small packages. Fine work can be done with sewing thread. It is the tightness of the tie, not the waterproofness of the binding that matters.

The best way to learn this craft is to work a sample of each of the various ties. It will quickly be discovered that even one tie pulls the fabric seriously out of shape. With a cluster of ties so much material is gathered up that a square yard of fabric may contract to 6 inches square whilst in its bindings. As with smocking, where the craftsman intends to arrange his ties in a regular order on the fabric, it is essential that he should mark it out before the first tie is made. The tied-up material may be dyed in any dye or vat, hot or cold. This is a white-on-black style, and the white will appear more brilliant if the background is dark. Indigo can hardly be surpassed.

Multi-colour effects can be produced by dyeing the fabric in successive baths of different colours. For example: tie up two-thirds of the fabric, and dye in colour A. Remove half of

96

the ties, leave the other half, and add a new set to fill the remaining third of the fabric. Dye in colour B, wash, and take off the ties. The result will be a dark background composed of colour B superimposed on colour A. The protected areas will show three colours, divided as follows: one-third will be colour B, one-third will be white, and one-third (where the last ties were put on) will be colour A.

A more subtle effect arises directly from the natural behaviour of dyes in solution. If two colours from the same dye family are mixed in the same dyebath, say a black and a yellow Direct dye, they will separate themselves where they meet the tied-up parts of the fabric. One will travel further than the other by capillary attraction, and will succeed in invading the protected areas for some distance. The result when the ties are removed will be a zone of white surrounded by a halo of the more active of the two colours, the whole set in a dark background of the two colours combined.

The ties must be left on until the dye has been fixed, whatever the fixing may be. In some cold recipes fixation is by immersion in a developing solution, in others by steam. Where steam is used, the fabric need not be wrapped in newspaper or scrim (open weave jute), as there is no danger of offsetting.

Ties made on thick fabrics give a slightly different effect from the same ties made on thin. If fine muslin is used, it can be folded double or even four times, and the ties made over two or four thicknesses at once. The following selection of ties is by no means exhaustive.

1 Place a small pebble behind the fabric, drape the fabric over it in the form of a small bell tent. Tie a collar tightly round the tent, as close up under the pebble as possible. Rubber bands do this quicker than raffia. If dried peas are used instead of pebbles, they may swell in the dyebath and burst the fabric. Or mice may gnaw them.

2 Begin as before, only before putting on the tie cover the outside of the fabric where it lies over the pebble with a small piece of waterproof sheeting (plastic, rubber, etc.).

3 Begin as before, and tie below the first collar any number of additional collars, some broad, some narrow.

4 Make a cluster of three or more pebbles, tied as in 1, as close together as possible. Regard the cluster as if it were one pebble at the apex of a tent, and tie a collar just under it.

5 Take a matchstick, hold it horizontally, and fold the fabric over it as if it were a pebble. Tie a collar underneath it. Now bind raffia round and round the enclosed match, beginning at the centre and working out to the two ends.

6 Fold up the fabric into narrow pleats running the whole length of the material. Regard the pleated fabric as a rope, and tie it in an ordinary overhand knot, or a chain of knots.

7 Pleat the fabric as before, and bind it round at intervals with ties, some broad, some narrow. All these pleating methods are best done on fine muslin.

8 Pleat the fabric as before in narrow pleats running the whole length of the material. Then, beginning at one end, fold up the pleat itself into a short concertina, or jack-in-the-box. Tie this together with a single band of raffia, as if tying up a square parcel.

9 This beautiful effect will only succeed on fine muslin. Pleat the fabric into three or four broad pleats running the whole length of the material. Now twist the material as if making it into a rope, and bind it round very tightly at frequent intervals.

10　Thread a needle with raffia or thread, and tie a very large knot at the opposite end. Draw a guiding line on the fabric, and sew along it with tacking stitches something less than a quarter of an inch long. After every inch or so, press the material back along the thread so as to compress it against the knot. The success of this method depends on this compression.

11　Draw a guide line on the fabric, and fold the fabric on the line. Fold over again to a depth of about half an inch. Fasten down the double fold with oversewing, pulling the thread tight.

12 · Batik

Java is the home of batik; the name comes from the Javanese word *tik*, meaning a fine point, a point of light in the dark. The Javanese believe that their art was brought to them by the Hindus – from Turkey and Egypt, they say, perhaps from Persia. Originally an aristocratic occupation, it was practised at home by the daughters of noble families. The work was entirely freehand, and required endless patience; months were spent on the production of a single piece. Batik printing began in about 1840 with the development of a special type of copper block known as 'tjap'. Commercial batik printing in Java today is organized as a village industry, each centre having its own fashion, but all strongly traditional.

Batik is one of the so-called resist styles of dyeing. The design is applied to the white fabric by means of some dye-resisting substance – in this case melted wax. The fabric is then immersed in a cold dyebath which dyes the background but is unable to dye the protected areas. Finally, the resisting substance is removed, and the design emerges as white against a dark background.

It is not likely that any European amateur will attempt to make a set of 'tjaps', or the little copper feeder called 'tjanting' used by the Javanese ladies to apply the wax. An enthusiast might like to make the primitive fountain pen used for the same purpose on the Coromandel coast.

FIG 17　Wax fountain pen

The nib consists of mild steel enclosed in a cocoon of hair, the handle is bamboo. Most amateurs use a brush, hoghair rather than sable.

Beeswax, rosin and paraffin wax (candles) are all used in batik, the choice depending on the designer's intentions. One of the charms of batik is an accidental effect resembling marble. This appears when a brittle wax is used. As the fabric is handled, the coating of wax breaks into an irregular network of hair cracks through which the dye finds its way. Paraffin wax is brittle. A mixture of about 4 parts rosin to 1 part paraffin wax is less brittle. Beeswax is sticky and leathery.

The best and safest way to heat wax is by electricity. Wax is a non-conductor of electricity. A useful heater can be improvised from two tins, and a 25-watt light bulb acting as an immersion heater.

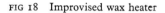

FIG 18   Improvised wax heater

The space between the inner and outer tin is filled with felt lagging. Wax is shredded with an old knife, and packed round the light bulb. The flex (cord) is tied with string to the outside tin to prevent the bulb from being accidentally jerked out when the heater is moved. An electrically heated glue pot also makes a good wax heater. The advantage of both these heaters is that they can be moved about as the work proceeds. The craftsman never need carry his loaded brush further than 6 inches, and in this distance the wax hardly has time to chill. Moreover, there is no risk of fire.

Batik can be dyed in any of the cold dyes and, as it is a light-on-dark style, the darker the background the better. Multi-colour effects are possible by immersing the fabric in a succession of dyebaths of different colours. Between each bath and the next the material is left to dry out thoroughly, and additional areas of wax are applied.

The craftsman now faces the tedious and unpleasant task of removing the wax. The wax itself is valuable and if it can be recovered it can be used again, even though coloured. To recover the wax, boil the fabric in soft water and skim off the wax as it rises to the surface.

This is the Javanese way. If the recovery of the wax is unimportant, it can be removed by ironing. Spread out the fabric on several thicknesses of newspaper, and lay more newspaper on top. Ironing the top layer will melt the wax and drive it into the newspaper. By changing the newspaper for fresh as often as it becomes saturated, most of the wax can be removed. The remainder can be cleared by washing the fabric several times in very hot water to which a little Stergene or Teepol (U.K.), Duponol or Synthrapol (U.S.A.) has been added. Despite all this effort it is almost impossible to get rid of the very last trace, and all true batik can be identified by a slight but unmistakable feel and smell of wax.

13 · Starch resists

Wax is only one of many substances used in resist-dye work; probably the most widely used is starch paste.

The Yoruba people of Nigeria excel in a style where the white fabric is decorated with cassava paste resist and then dyed in the indigo vat. Their designs are vigorous, and charged with symbolic meaning. The cassava paste is usually applied hot, either freehand, or through

FIG 19   Japanese stencil

a stencil punched out of sheet metal. Cassava is unobtainable in England or the United States, but an imitation can be made as follows:

$\frac{1}{2}$ oz	laundry starch
1 oz	ground rice
1 oz	plain white flour
$\frac{1}{2}$ pint (10 ozs)	hot water

Mix the ingredients to a smooth, stiff paste with a little cold water.

Add $\frac{1}{2}$ pint (10 ozs) hot water, stirring briskly to make a smooth cream.

Boil in a double saucepan for about thirteen minutes, stirring occasionally.

Apply hot, and leave to dry really hard before immersing in the vat.

There is no shortage of secret recipes for resists made from British gum and kaolin.

The difficulties begin when the fabric is put in the dyebath. All these recipes are made with water and, even though cold dyes are used, the paste becomes soft on immersion. Some way of preventing the fabric from rubbing against itself has to be found. The best way is to wind it on to a 'star' frame, such as the one made by the Macclesfield Engineering Company. Failing this a primitive winchbeck (roller) can be made. Stitch the two ends of the fabric together to form an endless band like a roller towel, starch side out. Arrange two broomsticks as rollers to run parallel with each other with a space of 12 or 18 inches between. Set these rollers at such a height so that when the fabric is hung over them, the bottom of the loop will just clear the bottom of a galvanized iron bath. Pour dye into the bath and pull the fabric round and round the rollers until dyeing is complete.

The continuous belt technique is ideally suited to indigo dyeing. As it is pulled over the rollers, the fabric passes first through the vat and then through the air, and the cycle is repeated over and over again. For starch resist work, the zinc-lime vat is the best recipe: it will build up to a warm bronzy-blue without destroying the resist. Care must be taken that the fabric passes well above the layer of sediment at the bottom of the vat.

At the end of the dyeing period, the fabric should be lifted and run round and round in the air until oxidation is uniformly complete. It should then be 'soured' by a short immersion in a bath of very dilute hydrochloric acid. The starch is removed by ordinary washing in hot water: several changes of water will be needed. Ironing will bring up the bronze lustre.

14 · Painting and drawing

If for any reason it is not possible to apply a dye from a dyebath it may be possible to paint it on to the fabric, and fix it afterwards by steam. For example, the amateur who is interested in resist styles, but daunted by the practical difficulties, will be able to produce something roughly in the batik manner by the following very simple method:

1 Paint the resist pattern on to the white fabric, using a mixture of plain white flour and cold water pasted to the consistency of condensed milk. Leave to dry hard.
2 Dissolve

1 oz	household dye
1 oz	glycerine, in
1 pint (20 ozs)	boiling water

Leave to cool.

Add just sufficient thickening to prevent spreading in the fibres by capillary attraction.

(This is no more than a simplified version of the direct dye printing recipe.)

With a distemper or paint brush, brush this solution over the flour-resisted side of the fabric.

Leave to dry.

3 Roll up the fabric and steam for one hour. Newspaper wrapping is not necessary.
4 Wash off.

This method works with other classes of dye; in fact any recipe that is suitable for printing is also suitable for freehand painting. Indigo, unfortunately, must be dyed in the classic manner, from a vat.

The flour-paste resist can be applied in several ways:
1 Freehand painting.
2 Stencilling.
3 Piped through a forcing bag, icing syringe, or slip tracer.
4 Spread as a thin, even film ready for paste combing. In this style, a pattern is made by scraping away the paste, while still wet, with a variety of combs.

Flour paste dries as a brittle crust, and if the fabric is crumpled before the colour is applied, the network of cracks will give a marbled texture resembling that found in batik.

Screen printing enthusiasts like to think that their craft altogether supersedes the primitive stencil, but this is not so. None of the wax or starch resists can be used in the screen, and yet the stencil handles them all without difficulty.

In one tradition the stencil shows how it can stand midway between controlled and freehand painting. The housewife in colonial America used to decorate her home with stencils. These were known as 'theorems', and consisted of zinc sheets ready punched with the elements from which a design could be built up. A favourite subject was a basket of fruit. The theorem on this subject would include, say, one basket, one peach, one apple, one grape, and three leaves of different shapes. The elements could be arranged and coloured at will, and the colouring could include any amount of gradation within the area of the perforation.

In truly freehand painting, the designer can please himself. He can use any kind of brush from the smallest sable to the largest whitewash brush, and he can also use the spray gun. Any of the printing recipes can be used. The thickening should be somewhat thinner than for block printing, but this must be decided by preliminary trial. The finished material must be given the fixation treatment appropriate to the recipe used.

The one thing that none of the orthodox hand processes can do is to print a long unbroken line: the joints between the separate prints always show. From time to time every designer will want to design stripes, and he will naturally want to see them on the fabric. The unorthodox technique sometimes known as tin printing solves the problem.

Stretch the fabric out on the table, and fasten down all round with Sellotape (U.K.) or masking tape (U.S.A.). Take a small tin and remove top and bottom carefully so as to leave a smooth rim. Stand the tin upright on the table just beyond one end of the fabric, and fill it with printing colour made to a thin screen-printing consistency. Grasp the tin firmly and, making sure that the bottom edge is not lifted, draw it along the fabric. Wherever it goes it will leave behind a perfectly even, thin trail of printing colour. To make long, straight lines a long deal batten (or wood strip) may be laid on the fabric as a guide rail. When the first stripe is dry a second may be superimposed, and where two stripes cross each other there will be a double thickness of colour. In this way it is very easy to produce checks.

Caution

Fabric printing is not a dangerous occupation, and the processes described in this book can be and are practised without harm year after year in schools and private homes. Nevertheless there are inherent dangers, and the craftsman must know where they are.

Chemicals

All chemicals must be stored under lock and key. Some are poisonous, others corrosive. The work bench and all utensils must be washed after use.

Particular care is needed when making solutions of caustic soda, quicklime and sulphuric acid. When any of these chemicals comes into contact with water, heat is generated. If done wrongly, corrosive splashes may be thrown several feet, and the container may crack.

The safe procedure is as follows:

1 Work near, but not in a sink.
2 Wear rubber gloves, apron, eye shield if available, otherwise keep the head well up.
3 Use a container made of Pyrex oven glass, glazed ceramic, plastic or enamel. Do not use metal.
4 Stand the container in a plastic bowl in which there is an inch or two of cold water.
5 Add the chemical to the water, a little at a time. Never pour water on the chemical.
6 Stir gently with a wooden stick.

If the skin is splashed, flood the place immediately with cold running water. If the eye is splashed, run to the sink and hold the eye open under running water for at least one minute. Consult a doctor as soon as possible.

Burns

Skin burns and scalds may result from handling the steam apparatus, and from spilling boiling liquids.

Carelessness and clumsiness are the chief cause. Use laundry tongs, oven gloves and aprons. Burns may be covered with dry dressings. If the clothes are drenched with boiling water, they must be taken off at once.

Cuts

Learn the correct use of all cutting tools, and keep them sharp. Cut fingers are caused by blunt tools.

Work on a firm bench and in a good light. Never attempt to cut in the lap.

The British and American Red Cross and such organizations as the St John Ambulance Brigade have an excellent handbook on First Aid.

Keep a First Aid box in the workshop.

Weights and measures

1 imperial gallon =	160 fluid ozs
1 litre =	34 fluid ozs
1 imperial pint =	20 fluid ozs
8 level teaspoons (U.K.) ⎫	
6 level teaspoons (U.S.A.) ⎬ =	1 fluid oz
2 level tablespoons ⎭	
1 imperial pint of water weighs	20 ozs avoirdupois
3 English pennies weigh	1 oz avoirdupois
2 English halfcrowns weigh	1 oz avoirdupois
1 English halfpenny weighs	$5\frac{1}{2}$ grams
1 English penny weighs	$9\frac{1}{2}$ grams
1 gram =	0·035 oz
1 oz =	28·35 grams
1 imperial pint =	0·567 litre
1 gallon (U.S.A.) =	128 fluid ozs
1 pint (U.S.A.) =	16 ozs
1 oz water weighs	1 oz avoirdupois
1 fluid oz =	0·0296 litre
1 cc water weighs	1 gram
1 cc =	0·338 fluid oz
$\dfrac{\text{grams per litre}}{100} =$	lbs per imperial gallon
$\dfrac{\text{grams per litre}}{6\cdot25} =$	ozs per imperial gallon
lb per imperial gallon $\times 100 =$	grams per litre
ozs per imperial gallon $\times 6\cdot25 =$	grams per litre

Centigrade to Fahrenheit
Multiply by 9, divide by 5, add 32
Fahrenheit to Centigrade
Subtract 32, multiply by 5, divide by 9

Bibliography

ARRANGED CHRONOLOGICALLY
Some of the earlier books will be found only in libraries.
The standard textbook is Knecht & Fothergill.

BANCROFT, E. *Experimental Researches Concerning the Philosophy of Permanent Colours; and the Best Means of Producing Them, by Dyeing, Calico Printing, etc* 2 vols, London, 1813

CROOKES, W. *A Practical Handbook of Dyeing and Calico Printing* Longmans Green, London, 1874

CRACE-CALVERT, F. *Dyeing and Calico Printing* Simpkin Marshall, London, 1876

SANSONE, A. *The Printing of Cotton Fabrics* Simpkin Marshall, London, 1887

BAKER, G. P. *Calico Painting and Printing in the East Indies in the XVII and XVIII Centuries* 2 vols, (text and plates), Edward Arnold, London, 1921

HUNTON, W. G. *English Decorative Textiles* John Tiranti, London, 1930

LEWIS, F. *English Chintz* Benfleet, Essex, 1935

TROTMAN, S. R., and TROTMAN, E. R. *The Bleaching, Dyeing and Chemical Technology of Textile Fibres* Charles Griffin, London, 1948

LAWRIE, L. G. *A Bibliography of Dyeing and Textile Printing (1510–1946)* Chapman & Hall, London, 1949

HORSFALL, R. S., and LAWRIE, L. G. *The Dyeing of Textile Fibres* Chapman & Hall, London, 1949

TAUSSIG, W. *Screen Printing* Clayton Aniline Co, Manchester, 1950

FLETCHER, F. M. *Wood-Block Printing* Sir Isaac Pitman, London (no date)

DESIRENS, L. *The Chemical Technology of Dyeing and Printing* 2 vols, Reinhold Publishing Co, New York, 1951

KORNREICH, E. *Introduction to Fibres and Fabrics* The National Trade Press, London, 1952

KNECHT, E., and FOTHERGILL, J. B. *The Principles and Practice of Textile Printing* Charles Griffin, London, 1912, 1924, 1936, 1952

VYDRA, J. *Indigo Blue Print in Slovak Folk Art* Artia, Prague, 1954

IRWIN, J. *Shawls. A Study in Indo-European Influences* H.M.S.O., London, 1955

COCKETT, S. R., and HILTON, K. A. *Basic Chemistry of Textile Colouring and Finishing* Philosophical Library, New York, 1956

SPEEL, HENRY C., and SCHWARZ, E. W. K. *Textile Chemicals and Auxiliaries* Reinhold Publishing Co, New York, 1957

HALL, A. J. *A Handbook of Textile Dyeing and Printing* The National Trade Press, London, 1955

ANON *Procion Dyestuffs in Textile Printing* Imperial Chemical Industries Ltd, London, 1960

CHAI FEI, HSU CHEN-PENG, CHENG SHANG-JEN and WU SHU-SHENG *Indigo Prints of China* Foreign Languages Press, Peking, 1956

Journal of Indian Textile History Articles in Vol II (1956), Vol III (1957), Calico Museum of Textiles, Ahmedabad

BUNT, C. G. E., and ROSE, E. A. *Two Centuries of English Chintz, 1750–1950* Leigh-on-Sea, 1957

STEINMANN, A. *Batik. A Survey of Batik Design* Leigh-on-Sea, 1958

BIEGELEISEN, J. I., and COHN, MAX ARTHUR *Silk Screen Techniques* Dover Publications, New York, 1958

HALL, A. J. *The Standard Handbook of Textiles* The National Trade Press, London, 1959

JAPAN TEXTILE COLOR DESIGN CENTER *Textile Designs of Japan* Osaka, Vol I (1959), Vol II (1960), Vol III (1961)

HIETT, H. L., and MIDDLETON, H. K. *Silk Screen Process Production* Blandford Press, London, 1960

TROWELL, M. *African Design* Faber & Faber, London, 1960

KOSLOFF, ALBERT *The Art and Craft of Screen Process Printing* The Bruce Publishing Co, New York, 1960

COCKETT, S. R., and HILTON, K. A. *Dyeing of Cellulosic Fibers and Related Processes* Academic Press, New York, 1961

ERICKSON, JANET *Block Printing on Textiles* Watson-Guptill Publications Inc, New York, 1961

LENNOX-KERR, P. (Edit) *Index to Man-Made Fibres of the World.* Man-made Textiles, Manchester, 1961

BLACKSHAW, H., and BRIGHTMAN, R. *Dictionary of Dyeing and Textile Printing* George Newnes, London, 1961

CARR, FRANCIS *A Guide to Screen Process Printing* Studio Vista Limited, London, 1961

ONIONS, W. J. *Wool, An Introduction to its Properties, Varieties, Uses and Production* Ernest Benn, London, 1962

DENNY, GRACE G. *Fabrics* J. B. Lippincott Co., Philadelphia, 1962

BIEGELEISEN, J. I. *Silk Screen Printing Production* Dover Publications Inc, New York, 1963

LAUTERBURG, LOTTI *Fabric Printing* Rheinhold Publishing Co, New York, 1963; B. T. Batsford, London, 1963

British suppliers

'MANUTEX'
Alginate Industries Ltd,
Walter House, Bedford St,
London WC2

DURAND & HUGUENIN'S CHROME COLOURS; 'EMULOSE B';
'INDIGOSOL' DYESTUFFS
Bard & Wishart,
Parkside Rd,
Sale, Cheshire

DYESTUFFS
CIBA Clayton Ltd,
Manchester

'TINOLITE' PIGMENT COLOURS
Geigy (Holdings) Ltd,
Civic Centre Rd,
Manchester 22

CHEMICALS, THICKENINGS, WAX
Gould, Thomas & Co,
Albert Rd,
Keynsham, Somerset

MINIMUM 5-LB LOTS OF ANY ONE DYESTUFF
I.C.I. Dyestuffs Division,
Hexagon House,
Blackley, Manchester 9

SEASONED WOOD BLOCKS; TOOLS AND MATERIALS FOR
BLOCK MAKING; FLOCKING
T. N. Lawrence & Son,
2 Bleeding Heart Yard, Greville St,
Hatton Garden, London EC1

SCREEN PRINTING EQUIPMENT, including tables, table
coverings, screen frames, squeegees, rubber strip;
small steamers; 'Star' frames
Macclesfield Engineering Co Ltd,
Athey St,
Macclesfield, Cheshire

'POLYPRINT' PIGMENT COLOURS
M. E. McCreary & Co,
21 Prince Edward Drive,
Belfast

SCREEN PRINTING EQUIPMENT, including 'Profilm',
bolting silk, organdie
Selectasine Silk Screens Ltd,
22 Bulstrode St,
London W1

'DYLON' DYES IN I-LB TINS; 'PROCION' DYESTUFFS
Mayborn Products Ltd,
Dylon Works,
Sydenham, London SE26

DYESTUFFS; MORDANTS; THICKENINGS
Skilbeck Brothers Ltd,
Bagnall House, 55 and 57 Glengall Rd,
London SE15

WOOD CARVING TOOLS; CRAMPS; MALLETS; PLASTERERS'
SCRIM; BEESWAX; PARAFFIN WAX; ROSIN
Alec Tiranti Ltd,
72 Charlotte St,
London W1

FAST BLACK; CHROMIUM ACETATE AND OTHER TWADDELL
SOLUTIONS; 'GLYDOTE B'; THICKENINGS; CHEMICALS
Youngs of Leicester Ltd,
40–42 Belvoir St,
Leicester

American suppliers

'KELTEX'
Kelco Co,
75 Terminal Ave,
Clark, New Jersey

'TINOLITE' PRODUCTS; 'REACTONE' AND OTHER DYE-
STUFFS
Geigy Chemical Co,
P.O. Box 430,
Yonkers, New York

'CIBACRON' AND OTHER DYESTUFFS
Ciba Chemical & Dye Co,
Fairlawn, New Jersey

CHEMICALS; THICKENINGS; WAX
Berg Chemical Co,
441 West 37th St,
New York, New York

'SITOL'; 'DUPONOL'; DYESTUFFS
E. I. du Pont de Nemours & Co,
Wilmington, Delaware

WOOD BLOCKS; TOOLS AND MATERIALS FOR BLOCK
MAKING
J. Johnson,
51 Manhasset Ave,
Manhasset, New York

SCREEN PRINT TABLES; TABLE COVERINGS; STEAMERS
Print Tables & Equipment Corporation,
765 Greenwich St,
New York, New York

SCREEN PRINTING SUPPLIES, including 'Nu-Film',
bolting silk, organdie, squeegees
Standard Supply Co,
54 West 21st St,
New York, New York

'PROCION' DYESTUFFS; 'GLYDOTE B'; 'SYNTHRAPOL'
Arnold, Hoffman & Co Inc,
55 Canal St,
Providence, Rhode Island

'DOWICIDE A'
The Dow Chemical Co,
45 Rockefeller Plaza,
New York, New York

'CALGON'
Calgon Co,
271 Madison Ave,
New York, New York

'KROMOFAX'
Union Carbide Chemicals Co,
270 Park Avenue, New York, New York

'ACCO-LITE' COLORS AND BINDERS
American Crayon Co,
Sandusky, Ohio

'SYNTHRAPOL S.P.'
I.C.I. Organics Inc,
55 Canal St,
Providence, Rhode Island

General hardware supplies (glue, nails, staples, etc.)
may be purchased at any hardware retailer and
general art supplies (paper, brushes, tacks, etc.) may
be purchased from any art supply retailer.

Acknowledgements

The author would like to thank all who submitted material for reproduction; and the following who gave permission for reproductions: The Claremont School for Spastic Children, Bristol; Mrs June Barker; George and Margaret Bruce; Miss Phyllis Barron; Swanshurst Bilateral School, Birmingham; The Central School of Arts and Crafts, London; Edinburgh Weavers Limited; Hull Traders Limited; The West of England College of Art, Bristol; Miss Caroline Scott; Mrs Sheila Wright; Miss Diana Reeves; Mr Ian Harper; Mr Robin Thomas; Chapman & Hall Ltd; Matthew Arnold Secondary School, Oxford; Alec Tiranti Ltd; The Victoria and Albert Museum, London. He would also like to thank Richard Morling for the devoted care he gave to the photography

Index